Praise for
Now That I'm Called

This is the exact book that I have always wanted to give to my female students. Here is a book that includes a wonderful biblical exposition of the theme of a "call" to ministry, lots of biographical stories about women who have gone into ministry, and some great tips on how to find your place in the harvest of gospel workers. This is simply mandatory reading for anyone contemplating going to seminary or engaging in ministry.

MICHAEL F. BIRD (PhD, University of
Queensland), Lecturer in Theology at
Ridley College, Melbourne, Australia

Kristen Padilla discusses this important issue in the correct manner: from the Bible, with an emphasis on the Bible's original languages and contexts and a heart for ministry rather than controversy. This volume is much needed, as conservative, moderate, and liberal Christians all seem confused about the nature and importance of rigorous theological training for women who teach the Bible in homes, churches, and academic settings.

PAUL HOUSE, professor of divinity,
Beeson Divinity School

Kristen Padilla offers an encouraging and carefully written work to help women thoughtfully discern their calling, to consider what their calling might look like in practical ministry terms, and ways of preparation for that ministry. She surveys biblical women whose ministries testified to God's call in their lives and introduces contemporary women who illustrate the same work of God in today's contexts. Padilla handles the Biblical text carefully and responsibly, offering Christ-focused explanations without shying away from difficult texts. She is empathetic, methodical, and a wonderfully patient guide.

STEFANA DAN LAING, assistant professor of divinity and theological librarian, Beeson Divinity School

My first reaction to this book was how much I wish I had it when I felt called to ministry as a teenager! Its greatest strengths are the emphasis on the biblical view of calling and the examples of women serving in different ministerial contexts. Whether you are a woman who feels called or a mentor to women, this is a go-to resource to walk you through a vocational calling to ministry.

COURTNEY TROTTER, youth director, The Gathering Church, Durham, North Carolina

I'm always on the lookout for books that get beyond the debate to patiently and reasonably guide women through what the Bible says about their call to ministry. Kristen Padilla's Now That I'm Called is that book. It is not only what I will recommend to my students but also what I'll buy for my daughter.

JOSEPH R. DODSON (PhD, University of Aberdeen, Scotland), associate professor of biblical studies, Ouachita Baptist University

NOW THAT I'M CALLED

A GUIDE FOR WOMEN DISCERNING A CALL TO MINISTRY

KRISTEN PADILLA

ZONDERVAN

To my husband, Osvaldo, with all my love.

ZONDERVAN

Now That I'm Called
Copyright © 2018 by Kristen Padilla

This title is also available as a Zondervan ebook.

Requests for information should be addressed to:
Zondervan, *3900 Sparks Dr. SE, Grand Rapids, Michigan 49546*

Library of Congress Cataloging-in-Publication Data

Names: Padilla, Kristen, 1983-
Title: Now that I'm called : a guide for women discerning a call to ministry / Kristen Padilla.
Description: Grand Rapids, Michigan : Zondervan, [2018] | Includes bibliographical references.
Identifiers: LCCN 2018018507| ISBN 9780310532187 (softcover) | ISBN 9780310532194 (e-book)
Subjects: LCSH: Women clergy. | Women in Christianity. | Clergy—Appointment, call, and election.
Classification: LCC BV676 .P33 2018 | DDC 262/.14082—dc23 LC record available at https://lccn.loc.gov/2018018507

CONTENTS

CONTENTS

INTRODUCTION

GETTING STARTED ON THE JOURNEY OF MINISTRY

I wish I could tell you the day or the hour that God called me to ministry, but I cannot. The call didn't come to me like it did to Jeremiah, whose mouth God touched and said, "'I have put my words in your mouth'" (Jer. 1:9). Nor did it come to me like it did Paul, who encountered Jesus on a road and was commissioned by him to be an apostle (Acts 9:1–9; 22:6–11). My calling didn't come in a bright vision or by audible words booming from heaven. It was rather a call that intensified over the years of God pursuing me, aligning my desires to his, revealing to me the gifts of the Holy Spirit he had given me, calling me through Scripture, like 2 Timothy 3:14–5:5 and Ephesians 4:10–16, through other believers who affirmed the work of God they saw in me, and through prayer. Simply put, I could not shake an increasing desire from God to serve him in the ministry of his Word within the context of the church. This is my calling story.

SENSING GOD AT WORK

I remember crying to my mother, shortly after I became a Christian, "Why didn't God make me a boy so I could be a preacher?" Even at a young age, all I wanted to do was to proclaim the gospel the best way a seven-year-old preacher's daughter knew how: by preaching. My cry was the result of a clash between my God-given desire to proclaim the gospel and what I saw in my reality. The only people I encountered who had a formal ministry of the Word were men, and the only place I saw them exercise that ministry was in the pulpit. The two women I knew who had done any type of ministry —Annie Armstrong and Lottie Moon—were long dead, and they were missionaries.

At the first church my dad served as pastor, a small church in rural East Texas, he was the only full-time staff member. It wasn't until we moved to the "city" when I was in fifth grade, to a slightly larger church in Texarkana, Texas, that I became part of a church that had a full-time music and youth minister. My dad was now one of two ministers on staff. From time to time we would welcome a visiting missionary or evangelist, but for the most part, if you were in full-time ministry, you were either a senior pastor or music/youth pastor.

Being female in my denomination excluded me from at least the first ministry option and most likely the second, and even if the church had accepted women in those roles, God was not leading me to those ministries. So I considered whether God was calling me to become a missionary, and if he was, whether he was calling me to be a foreign missionary. I was afraid of going overseas or starting a church in a remote village. (As you can see, even my understanding of missions and being a missionary was limited.) I didn't know what to do, but even though I could not figure out a specific role or ministry God was calling me to do, I could not shake my increasing desire to serve God full-time in some way.

So for two years, from ages thirteen to fifteen, I struggled with whether God was calling me to serve him as something other than a lay person. I allowed fear, the voices of others, and what I saw in my little piece of the world to be deterrents to my pursuit of gospel ministry. I had no books to read about being a young woman called to ministry. There was no one in my life—no woman doing full-time ministry—who could mentor me. I felt like I was traveling down a road where no one had ventured before. It was unfamiliar territory, and I had no one to guide me.

Even though I felt alone, God was still pursuing me. In the summer between my ninth and tenth grade years, at a weeklong discipleship camp targeted for Christian leaders of youth groups, I finally surrendered to the call to commit my life to a ministry of the Word for the church. The specific direction was unclear, but I knew God was at work.

I had been reflecting on something my mother told me about obedience: "Kristen," she'd say, "if Jesus is the Lord of your life, then you obey and trust him whether or not you can see the complete picture or the final outcome. You will not be at peace until you release your future, your ambitions, and your fears to the Lord and surrender to his call." One night at camp, I simply surrendered. My prayer went something like this: "Here I am, God. Use me. I am yours. I am yours to use in your church, for your people. I don't know what that will look like, but I will trust you."

Naively, I believed that because I had surrendered, God would reveal what "ministry" would look like for the rest of my life. He didn't. I believed life would be easier since I had been "chosen" for ministry. It wasn't. (In fact, I struggled with sin, temptation, and doubt more during my last two years of high school than I had in my entire life!) I also believed God would not abandon me and that he would carry out his purposes in my life. And those two things, he did.

After I graduated from high school, I attended Ouachita Baptist University in Arkadelphia, Arkansas. I chose the school because it had a reputable Christian studies degree geared toward preparing future ministers of the gospel. I had a great experience during my time at Ouachita, but I still did not have clarity about what my specific ministry should be. Rather, keeping with the way he had been working in my life for so many years, God was slowly, in small, quiet ways, affirming my gifts and revealing his plan. During my time in college, God opened doors for me to communicate his Word through writing, mentoring, teaching, and speaking. Professors and fellow students continued to affirm my gifts. I was even asked to give my testimony during Ouachita's weekly chapel service during my senior year. God used moments such as these, along with my professors and peers, to further affirm my call.

The professors at Ouachita did an outstanding job of teaching Scripture and giving students tools to be competent biblical interpreters, but this only whetted my appetite for more theological education. It was around this time that I sensed God directing me to go to seminary. I wanted to pursue further studies because I believed my calling was a high calling. It meant I would speak about the living God, and I needed the best training possible to do it well.

In August 2005, I made the seven-hour journey from my home in Sheridan, Arkansas, to Birmingham, Alabama, to attend Beeson Divinity School for a master of divinity (MDiv) degree. During my season of study at Beeson, other people continued to affirm my gifts in writing and speaking, and God also continued to kindle the desire to teach his Word. In particular, as I worked with young women at my local church, God put a desire in my heart to help them process what it means to be called by God for ministry.

WHERE I AM TODAY

When I graduated from seminary in 2008 with my MDiv, no work seemed to be available for me in ministry. The economy was in very poor shape. People were losing jobs, and churches were under hiring freezes. I started a blog as a place to write about God's Word, took an internship at a Baptist newspaper, got married, and had a son. For four years I was a stay-at-home mom learning what it meant to worship God through the mundane tasks of household chores as well as the awesome responsibility of raising a child in the fear of the Lord. During that time, I wrote a couple of Bible studies for publication. God gave me opportunities to lead retreats, preach his Word at women's events, teach adult Sunday school classes, and mentor women who felt called to ministry. Today I am realizing my calling in writing this book. God gave me the initial vision for this book ten years ago, and I am eager for it to be in the hands of young women like you who feel called to ministry.

In May 2015, almost seven years after I graduated from seminary, I went to work at Beeson Divinity School. While the job itself is not what I would consider gospel ministry, it does allow me to do some ministry of the Word for the church. How? Each semester I am tasked with taking the theme of our semester-long chapel series and translating that theme into a devotional booklet that is sent to around three thousand people. I give vision to, create, write for, and edit a new devotional booklet twice a year. I also mentor young women in seminary.

Around the same time I took the job at Beeson, my husband and I changed denominations, moving from a Southern Baptist church to an evangelical Episcopal church in the Anglican tradition. At the time of the writing of this book, I am in conversations with the clergy about the possibility of formal ministry within my new denomination.

You would think that in the eighteen years since I surrendered to ministry at camp, I would have figured it all out and that God would have revealed to me all there is to know about my calling and what he plans to do with me. But that's not so. I have had to learn, like many people in the Bible did, to trust God even though I cannot see the end result or exactly where he is taking me. *I have learned that the call is a journey.*

I am sharing my calling story with you so you can see that calling is fluid. It takes different shapes and sizes along the way. However, I also want you to see that while my life and work have evolved, God and his call to deliver his Word has been sure and steady. He who has called me is faithful. God isn't asking us to be in control of our callings or to make them look like what *we* want them to look like. Rather, he is asking us to be obedient and trust him every step of the way, knowing that he is always faithful. Besides, it is not about us, is it? It is about God receiving all the glory (2 Cor. 4:7).

I am still on the journey. I have had to learn what it means to trust and depend on God. Although there have certainly been times of confusion and disappointment, I have never regretted the journey nor looked back. This is my calling story. What is yours?

INITIAL THOUGHTS ON CALLING

Before we go any further, I'd like to suggest that you take a moment to write out a few thoughts about your own calling story. How do you sense God calling you to ministry? How are others affirming you in this call? What are some of your struggles with your calling? Where are you right now in your journey?

WHAT IS "VOCATIONAL MINISTRY"?

Whenever I speak to women about the question of calling, several questions frequently come up:

- What do you mean by the words *calling* and *ministry*?
- Isn't everyone called to ministry? Are you saying that some people are called to a ministry of the gospel that is somehow *different* from the call God has placed on every Christian?

These are great questions. I'll start by defining for you what I mean by *calling* and *ministry*. This is important because whenever I refer to ministry in this book, I'm not using the term in the broad sense that all Christians are called to engage in service. Instead, I'm using the term in the colloquial sense—calling as vocational ministry, typically involving some form of teaching or preaching role. So whenever I speak about a "call to ministry" I'm referring to vocational ministry. A call to vocational ministry can best be understood as God setting someone apart to serve him, for the good of his people, by delivering the Word of God (in some way) to them. Keep this in mind. It's important!

One of the reasons I'm writing this book is because I want people, especially women, to understand that receiving this kind of call does *not* mean that they must hold a church office—the role of a pastor, elder, or deacon, for example. The Holy Spirit gives gifts to the people of God, and these gifts can be exercised outside of a particular office in the church. Ministering God's Word in this way is a valid, biblical calling. The Bible frequently speaks about gifts of prophecy, teaching, and exhortation, and as I will argue later, these terms are best understood as referring to the teaching and preaching of the Word. God does not restrict these gifts to people who hold ordained offices in the church, and as we will see in later chapters, nowhere in the context of biblical teaching on these gifts is this limitation required (Rom. 12:3–8; 1 Cor. 12:4–11, 27–31).

In addition to clarifying what I mean by *ministry*, I want to unpack what we mean when we talk about a *calling*. Many people are confused by the word *calling*. One reason is that the term is used in several different ways in the Bible. One way it is used is in reference to a divine directive we receive from God—God is calling us to do something. But many different kinds of calls exist within this broad understanding of what God is asking us to do. Scripture even uses different words and phrases to express a call from God, words like *set apart, send, appoint,* or *commission*. In addition, the Bible most often uses the word *calling* to speak of God calling men and women into relationship with himself (Rom. 1:6–7; Eph. 4:1; 2 Tim. 1:8–9; 1 Pet. 1:1–2, 15–16). We all share in this broader sense of being called by God. All those who place their faith in Jesus and respond to the good news of salvation are called to be God's children. All of us are called to some type of ministry—called to serve God in some way.

With this in mind, I want to clarify that the type of call I'm addressing in this book is more specific: the call some receive to a ministry of delivering God's Word for the benefit of the people of God. This kind of calling will necessarily involve *communicating* God's Word—whether that is through preaching, teaching, speaking, or writing—for the building up, equipping, and edifying of the church of Jesus Christ (Eph. 4:11–13). We'll talk more about this in chapter 6.

So how do you know if you are called to *this* kind of ministry? That's a good question! As we will see in the first four chapters of this book, the Bible reveals that throughout history, God has called a wide variety of people in many different ways. Some people have been called through direct speech, or through dreams and visions, or God has sovereignly used other people to make his call known to them. In the church today, God commonly calls his people through the personal reading of Scripture, in the context of a worshipping community where the Word is preached, and through prayer. God makes his call known through other believers as well, through people who see and recognize God's work in our lives. God also works internally within us, inclining our hearts and desires to respond to his call, and he works through the specific gifts he gives to us to serve others within the body of Christ. Finally, though I won't be addressing this, it's important to recognize that in many parts of the world today, God still calls people through dreams and visions.

More often than not, God uses a variety of means to call us to a ministry of the Word. However, a true call from God never originates from within ourselves. God's call comes from *outside* us and then reorients our hearts and desires in such a way that, like Paul (1 Cor. 9:16), we are then compelled to serve in a specific type of ministry. Speaking about the call of the Old Testament prophets, theologian Brevard Childs writes, "A strong sense of *divine compulsion* lay at the heart of the call" (emphasis mine).[1] What Childs means is that when we sense God's call, we cannot think of doing anything else! God's call is so convicting and convincing that it takes over our hearts and minds.

Theologian Thomas Oden, writing about how to discern a call to vocational ministry, said the following: "Let an initial impression grow quietly in a community of prayer until it becomes a sustained conviction."[2] God speaks to us in many ways, but over time a sense of calling will grow into a certain conviction. We need a process of discernment, a way of "testing" a call to see if it is really from God. We should start by comparing what we think God is calling us to against the truth God has revealed in Scripture. We should listen to what other believers are telling us, and we should think about our sense of calling in consideration of our spiritual gifts. Ask those around you: "What do you see God doing in my life? What do you see as my spiritual gifts?" How do people react when you tell them that you sense God is calling you to gospel ministry? We'll take a closer look at some of these questions throughout the book.

A MAP OF THIS BOOK

As you can see, I'll be trying to answer many questions for you! I want to be up-front with you as we get started, though. Two beliefs have guided me in writing this book. First, I believe that God calls women to ministry, and more specifically, to the type of ministry I described earlier—the ministry of communicating God's Word to God's people. Second, I believe that the church of Jesus Christ needs God-called women who are prepared and trained for this ministry. The specifics of what this type of "gospel" ministry looks like for you will largely depend on your tradition, your reading of Scripture, and where you sense God is leading you. But regardless of your church or tradition, I believe you have a place in ministry if God is calling you to serve.

Individualism and self-sufficiency make up the fabric of our culture. Today it doesn't really matter what your parents or grand-parents did; we each blaze our own trail. As we begin considering a call to ministry, we need to be aware that this individualism may be infused in our thinking. For example, you might be inclined to see your calling as an isolated event, thinking to yourself, *God called me, and I will pursue this on my own.* I can certainly relate to that! I didn't want to pursue my call to ministry on my own, but I couldn't find any women in the part of East Texas where I lived who sensed a similar call. I wrongly assumed that I was unique, that my calling was just between God and me. I learned the hard way that God's intention was never for us to do life alone. The same is true for you!

Instead of interpreting our callings individualistically, we need to think about them in light of two contexts: *history* and *community*. To put it simply, God is not going to call or act in a way that he hasn't already done in the past, and he is not going to gift us in a way that is different from how he has gifted others in the past. We can better understand and interpret our callings as we look back (in history) and look around us (at our community). We are not the entire puzzle that God is putting together; we are simply one *piece* of the puzzle.

The famous nineteenth-century philosopher and theologian Søren Kierkegaard said, and I'm paraphrasing here, "Life can only be understood backwards; but it must be lived forwards."[3] We'll start our journey by looking backward, to history. We do this so that we can think about our own sense of calling in light of the ways God has called people in the past and the purposes for which he called them. We will also look at how these people responded to their callings and ask ourselves what we can learn about our personal sense of calling in light of this.

The first two chapters will be framed around a question: *How does God call people to ministry and for what purposes?* We will survey individuals in Scripture whose calling stories and roles in the history of salvation can help refine our own understanding of calling and ministry. Their stories provide us with examples and principles of how God calls people to serve him. In the first chapter, we will focus on the Old Testament and consider four individuals: Moses, Joshua, David, and Jeremiah. You might wonder why I did not include a woman in this chapter. Don't worry! I will be discussing several female examples in chapter 3.

In the second chapter, we'll turn to the New Testament and look specifically at Jesus, Peter, Paul, and Timothy as examples. We'll also look at what the New Testament says about the call to vocational ministry—the ministry of communicating God's Word to God's people. The Bible contains so many examples of callings—in both the Old and New Testaments—that we won't be able to look at them all. So while the examples I've chosen are useful in establishing a biblical understanding of how and to what God calls people in ministry, I'd like to encourage you, after reading these first two chapters, to look at other examples as well.

After establishing what it means to be called by God in the first two chapters, I'll turn to the question that is the primary focus of this book: *If God is in the business of calling individuals for the gospel, what does that mean for me as a woman? Can a woman even be called to vocational ministry of the Word?* I'll unpack the answer to this in chapters 3 and 4 through a survey of the roles of women in Scripture and attempt to answer the following questions as well: Can we discern a pattern here concerning women? What kinds of observations can we make about the way God uses women in ministry? We will seek to answer these questions by looking most closely at Deborah and Huldah in the Old Testament (chapter 3), and then looking at Mary, the mother of Jesus, Priscilla, Phoebe, Junia, Elizabeth, Euodia, Syntyche, and those listed by Paul in Romans 16 as we turn to what the New Testament has to say (chapter 4).

Of course, it's not enough to simply look at examples of biblical figures, so I'll spend an entire chapter taking a close look at one of the most discussed New Testament passages referenced on this issue: 1 Timothy 2:11–15. Does this text prohibit women from being called to the type of vocational ministry I'm referring to? In chapter 5, we will examine this passage and ask if it supports or restricts women from certain types of ministry.

Chapter 6 serves as a hinge for the book, helping us to look both backward and forward. In this chapter we will address the question of spiritual gifts: What are they, and how does one receive them? We will study the spiritual gifts God gave people in the past for a Word-based ministry by considering Ephesians 4:11–13 and then ask if God gives those same gifts to us today. If the answer is yes, what might it look like to have the gift of prophecy or shepherding in ministry?

As we continue looking forward, the final two chapters show you how you can prepare yourself for ministry in light of what we've just studied in Scripture. In chapter 7, we will look at the importance of theological education for ministry. What is theological education and why is it important? How does one choose where to receive theological education? Finally, in chapter 8 we'll look at how you can get practical training through mentorships and internships. How do you choose or find a mentor? Where should you look for an internship, and what makes a good one?

To help you process through the material in each chapter in a way that is applicable and relevant, I have provided follow-up questions. My hope is that the Reflection Questions will be useful for personal reflection and further study, and the Discussion Questions will be used with a trusted mentor (if you have one). I've also included Personal Exercises you can do to further explore your own sense of calling as a woman.

I close each chapter by introducing you to a woman who has been called to and involved in one of the many varieties of gospel ministry. These ministry spotlights help us to see that each woman's calling is unique, and God can call a woman to serve him in today's church in a variety of ways. These women represent several Protestant evangelical denominations, and each one is living out her calling in a different context. I want you to meet these women so you can see you are not alone! Many opportunities are available to women in ministry, and I hope these women and their stories encourage you.

I realize this is a lot of ground to cover. I've heard it said that if something isn't difficult, it isn't worth doing. Pursuing your calling will be difficult at times, and I want to give you a guidebook that helps you embrace the long view. My hope is that this book will help you ground your calling in Scripture and the character of God and will assist you to be faithful to the end, wherever you are called to serve. I take your calling from the Lord seriously, and have attempted to write a guidebook that reflects that seriousness.

This book won't give you all the answers. It's not a playbook with secret plays that will help you win the game. It's not a step-by-step how-to book for securing a job or getting into seminary. Rather, this is a *guide*book. I want to guide you through the hard questions, through Scripture, and through some of the twists and turns that come with considering this type of call. The goal is for you to grow into maturity and deeper faithfulness in ministry.

WALKING TOGETHER ON THE JOURNEY

I consider it a joy and a privilege to walk with you through your calling journey. Even though I do not know you personally, I have been praying for you as you seek to understand what it is God has for you. Eighteen years ago, when I surrendered to God's call in my own life, I felt alone. I soon came to see that many women before me walked down a similar path. The more I looked and asked around, the more I discovered other young women my age around the world walking down the same path. I just didn't know about them at first!

Perhaps you've picked up this book because you feel alone. If so, I hope that by reading my story and the stories of others, you will find encouragement. Most importantly, I hope you will be reminded that God has never abandoned you, and he never will. As you discern and work out your calling, hold fast to the truth that the One who has called you is faithful. If you can trust him for your salvation, then you can trust him with your calling. So be encouraged by this word from the Lord: "God is faithful, who has called you into fellowship of his Son, Jesus Christ our Lord" (1 Cor. 1:7–9).

One of my friends, Rebecca, shared an email she had written to one of her professors while she was attending seminary. She was asking him for guidance regarding her life and ministry. She wrote:

> When I meditated on the word GUIDANCE, I kept seeing "dance" at the end of the word. I remember reading that doing God's will is a lot like dancing. When two people try to lead, nothing feels right. The movement doesn't flow with the music, and everything is uncomfortable and jerky. When one person realizes

that and lets the other lead, both bodies begin to flow with the music. One gives gentle cues, perhaps with a nudge to the back or by pressing lightly in one direction or another. It's as if the two become one body, moving beautifully. The dance takes surrender, willingness, and attentiveness from one person and gentle guidance and skill from the other. My eyes were drawn back to the word GUIDANCE. When I saw "G," I thought of God, followed by "u" and "i." "God, 'u' and 'i' dance." God, you and I dance. I became willing to trust that I would get guidance about my life. I became willing to let God lead. My prayer for you today is that God's blessings and mercies be upon you on this day and every day. May you abide in God as God abides in you. Dance together with God, trusting God to lead and to guide you through each season of your life . . . And I hope you dance![4]

I think Rebecca offers us all a great word as we begin this book. As we seek guidance about our calling and the ministries in which we serve, we must first surrender to God's lead and trust him to guide us on the journey.

> *May God use this study to prepare dynamic young women, like yourself, whom he is calling for a lifetime of ministry, so that you will be effective in reaching the world for Jesus Christ. Amen.*

REFLECTION QUESTIONS

1. Have you ever thought of calling as a long, complex process? Do you agree or disagree with that idea? Does it make you feel discouraged or relieved? Why?

2. Looking at your calling story, the one you wrote down earlier, can you see a pattern of God's faithfulness and affirmation in your life? If so, write down those points of faithfulness and affirmation.

3. What do you fear most in regard to your calling?

DISCUSSION QUESTIONS

I would encourage you to find a mentor who can help guide you in the process of discerning your calling. The following are suggested questions you can ask your mentor.

1. What is your calling story? (Share yours with her.)

2. What wisdom can you give me at the beginning of my calling journey?

3. How do you remain faithful when the calling journey gets tough?

PERSONAL EXERCISES

1. Write down your calling story, if you haven't already.

2. Read Genesis 12–20. Summarize Abraham's calling story. How did God call Abraham, and to what did he call him? What obstacles did Abraham overcome to remain faithful to God's calling on his life? Now read Hebrews 11:8–19. What is the testimony Scripture gives concerning Abraham?

CHAPTER 1

Calling in the Old Testament

Holy Scripture is a story about calling. It begins with a God who determined to have a people for himself and in relationship with himself. "In the beginning . . . God created mankind in his own image, in the image of God he created them; male and female he created them" (Gen. 1:1, 27). Ever since Adam and Eve sinned and as a result, were forced to leave the presence of God, God has been calling or wooing his people back to himself. The Bible tells us that, like the father who waits for the prodigal son and also urges the elder son to come join the party (Luke 15:11–31), God has been calling us back home and even going out to bring us back. He is the God who "freely wills not to be without us and wills to be with us."[1]

This is why the mission and heart of God can be summed up with a refrain we find throughout all of Scripture: "My dwelling place will be with them; *I will be their God, and they will be my people*" (Ezek. 37:27, emphasis mine). This is the reality we find at the beginning of creation, even before the fall. Scottish theologian T. F. Torrance says, "God is who he is as he who loves us with his very Being . . . interacting with us in creation and history, and in our human and physical existence in time and space, all to be our God and to have us for his people."[2] God has entered into our mess, and "moved into the neighborhood" (John 1:14, MSG). In Jesus Christ, we do not serve a far-off God, but a personal God who is near. What does the mission of God have to do with our callings? Everything! It is for this purpose—God wanting to have a people for himself— that God calls men and women, you and me, into "the ministry of reconciliation" (2 Cor. 5:18). We proclaim and point others to Jesus, who reconciles us to God.

How do we see this worked out in Scripture? From the very beginning, God calls individual people for special tasks. In Genesis 1, after creating the first man and woman, God blesses them and gives them a mandate—calling papers, if you will: "'Be fruitful and increase in number; fill the earth and subdue it. Rule over the fish in the sea and the birds in the sky and over every living creature that moves on the ground'" (Gen. 1:28). Old Testament scholar John Walton makes a compelling case that what we find in the second chapter of Genesis is *temple* and *priest* symbolism. Therefore, the garden is like a "cosmic temple," and Adam and Eve are quasi-priests in this "sacred space," serving God by caring for creation.[3]

After the fall, the narrative zooms in on certain individuals God calls for purposes within the divine plan of salvation: Noah and Abraham. Both are called to believe and to obey. They are promised things they cannot see: a flood (Noah) and a nation that outnumbers the stars (Abraham). As a result, Noah is to build an ark and gather animals, and Abraham is to travel throughout the land (Gen. 12:1, 4–10) and father a great nation (Gen. 18:18–19). Through Noah, God recreates creation and humanity; through Abraham, salvation comes to a people and thereby to the nations. We see repeatedly in Scripture that not only does God choose to have a people for himself, but he chooses to use individuals to call more people.

I want us to look at a select few of the people God used in the Old Testament, asking questions such as: How did God call them? For what purpose did he call them? What promises did God give them? What successes or troubles did they have in their callings? You may notice that all these individuals are men. Don't let this deter you. I believe we can learn much from how God calls people—men as well as women. I encourage you to keep your Bible nearby as you read this book, and to take time to read the passages of Scripture.

Let's get started!

THE CALL OF MOSES

The story of Moses is one of the most well-known in the Bible. This has its disadvantages because we might overlook some important details because of the story's over-familiarity. As we look at Moses, let's try to do so with fresh eyes.

Moses is one of a few people in the Old Testament for whom we are given a birth narrative (Ex. 1–2). Think of some of the Bible heavyweights about whose births we know few or no details. David, Daniel, Peter, and Paul are a few that come to mind. Why, then, does the Exodus story begin with Moses' birth and not with his calling? We are given details of Moses' beginning as a witness to God's providence over Moses (Heb. 11:23–28). What we see is how God is orchestrating the deliverance of his people long before "their cry for help because of their slavery went up to God" (Ex. 2:23). Moses is God's choice from the beginning, and nothing will stop God from using him, not even Pharaoh and his decree. By all accounts Moses should have been killed as a newborn with the thousands of other Hebrew baby boys; death is also a possibility when he is laid in a basket on the river; finally, death is a possibility when he flees Egypt and lives in exile. But nothing or no one will thwart God's plan.

In an ironic plot twist, Pharaoh's daughter is the one who rescues Moses and adopts him as her son. Not only does God thwart Pharaoh's plan, but he places Moses in Pharaoh's own household! God protects Moses when he is the most vulnerable, and when Moses is grown, he refuses to be known as the son of Pharaoh's daughter (Heb. 11:24).

Moses is God's servant, chosen to lead his people out of Egypt long before God speaks to Moses from the bush; and we see this in God's sovereignty over Moses' birth. (We will see this same theme resurface in Jeremiah and Paul.) When God eventually calls Moses to a task that will forever alter his life, he does so in a very peculiar way. God speaks to him from a bush that appears to be on fire yet is not consumed. Furthermore, he calls Moses by name.

The Response of Moses

Moses is not convinced that God has chosen the right person for the job. After his spectacular encounter with God, Moses' first response is "Who am I?" (Ex. 3:11). Moses doesn't see himself as fit for the task. He is not (or perhaps doesn't believe himself to be) an eloquent speaker. He says, "I am slow of speech and tongue" (Ex. 4:10). Moses is also worried he will not be believed (v. 1). Finally, Moses begs God not to send him (v. 13). Moses is aware of his inadequacies and is fearful. There's nothing in his flesh that wants to do the job God is calling him to do. What we see in Moses is someone who is very human, *someone like you, like me.*

Even now as I am writing this book, I often think of others who are more qualified than I am to write on this topic. I can think of many valid excuses for why I should not write this book. Often I ask God, like Moses, "Who am I?" to do this task. God answers Moses' question, "Who am I?" with a statement about who *God* is. Moses is correct: who he is *alone* is not going to cut it. But Moses' "I" is overruled by God's "I." God says, "'I will be with you'" (Ex. 3:12). The question is not who *is* Moses but who is *with* Moses. The Most Holy God, the God of the universe, is with him; this is what makes Moses qualified to do and go as God has commanded. In verse 13 Moses asks for God's name. God responds, "'I AM WHO I AM'" (v. 14). The "I AM WHO I AM" swallows up the "Who am I?"[4]

Knowing this truth, that, God qualifies us when he calls, sends, and goes with us, gave me the confidence to write this book. And I hope it gives you the confidence to follow him in whatever ministry he is calling you to. What am I by myself? Nothing. But when God calls us and is with us, we are able.

My friend Leslie Ann Jones, who ministers by communicating God's Word through teaching and writing, finds this part of Moses' story "deeply comforting." She says:

> Ultimately, my call and my work isn't about me at all. It's about the Lord. It's about who he is and what he can do. I'm limited

in nearly every possible way, but he is limitless. There have been times in my life when God has placed a task in my path that stops me in my tracks. In my heart, I rage against God and squirm against his plan. *I can't do this, God! What are you thinking? Why would you ask me to go there? To do that? Anything but that, Lord. Anything.* And every single time, he gently reminds me that when I can't, he can. My shortcomings only magnify his glory. And just like he was faithful to Moses all those years ago, he will be faithful to me here and now.[5]

Other details about Moses might make him an unlikely candidate in our minds, although he doesn't use these as excuses himself. Moses is an old man, in his eighties (Ex. 7:7), married with children, when God speaks to him from that bush. In a world where we believe we have to *do* and *have* it all by the time we are thirty, this part of Moses' story might come as a shock. We might rationalize it by saying, "Well, people lived longer back then." But Moses dies when he is around 120 years old (Deut. 34:7), which means he has lived two-thirds of his life before God calls him. Moses is also a murderer and an outcast (Acts 7:24–29). No longer a prince of Egypt nor accepted by his own kin, he is now simply a shepherd in the land of Midian.

However, neither Moses' past failures nor his status nor his age count him out. God chooses him not because Moses deserves or earns it, but because *God will be glorified through him.* God's strength will be displayed through Moses' weaknesses. When God responds to Moses' concerns, he wants Moses to see that the call is not dependent upon Moses' abilities but on God's abilities. As "servant of the LORD" (Deut. 34:5), he is simply called to serve and imitate God, the true Deliverer and Shepherd of the Hebrews.

Have you, too, made excuses to God about a call to ministry? Reread the above paragraph and substitute Moses' name with first-person pronouns. Like Moses', your call is dependent upon God's strength, abilities, and skills, not yours.

Moses' call is God-sized, which means only God can enable

Moses to fulfill it. It is a call with difficulties and dangers. But God is with Moses. Also, once Moses accepts the call, he will never return to his former way of life. He will never be the same.

The Ministry of Moses

God tells Moses he has heard the cries of his people and has "come down to rescue them" (Ex. 3:8). But just how is God going to deliver them? "I am sending you," God tells Moses (v. 10). God calls Moses to act on his behalf for his people as *deliverer* and *prophet*. God coming down to rescue his people is worked out through Moses.

As deliverer, Moses intercedes for the release of the Hebrews and leads them out of Egypt, through the Red Sea. As prophet, Moses delivers God's message to Pharaoh and to the Hebrews. Look how often the text says, "God spoke to Moses" or "The LORD said to Moses." A large part of Exodus is comprised of God communicating his word to Moses and Moses communicating that word to the people. In the New Testament, Stephen says of him: "He received living words to pass on to us" (Acts 7:38). This role of prophet does not stop with the deliverance of God's people but continues during the journey through the wilderness as God gives the Law and makes a covenant with his people through his *intermediary* Moses.

While deliverer and prophet constitute most of Moses' call, there is still more to it. Moses *governs* the people, mediating their disputes (Ex. 18:13–23) and speaking on their behalf to God. In many ways Moses is like a *shepherd* of the people, a role he knew well before his calling (Isa. 63:11; Ps. 77:20). Listen to how Moses describes his calling in Numbers 11 as he cries out to God when the people are complaining that they do not have any meat to eat:

> "Did I conceive all these people? Did I give them birth? Why do
> you tell me to carry them in my arms, as a nurse carries an infant,
> to the land you promised on oath to their ancestors?" (v. 12)

Moses uses this analogy to explain his reality. God has asked Moses to care for his people on his behalf as a nurse, or a mother, cares for a baby. These metaphors—shepherd and nurse—describe Moses as he governs and cares for God's people.

How Moses Fulfilled His Calling

God gives Moses at least two promises after commissioning him. The first is a promise of his presence. In Exodus chapters 3 and 4 (and again in chapters 33–34), there is a recurring promise: "I will be with you" or "I am with you." In Numbers 11:17, we are told that the Spirit of God is on Moses. Moses' call is God's call. God will see it through, and he will be with his servant.

The second promise concerns God's word. This promise is given as an answer to Moses' "what if" questions. When Moses asks, "What if they ask who is it who sent me? What shall I tell them?" (Ex. 3:13, paraphrased), God promises to give his word to Moses. In Exodus 4:12, God tells Moses, "'Now go; I will help you speak and will teach you what to say.'" Moses receives direct speech from God from the moment of his calling throughout the rest of his life. God's presence and word accompany Moses wherever he goes.

But even with God's presence and word, Moses' calling is difficult. The Hebrew people constantly complain and disobey Moses and God.[6] Stephen in the New Testament says of these people, "But our ancestors refused to obey him. Instead, they rejected him and in their hearts turned back to Egypt" (Acts 7:39). They make a golden calf when Moses is on the mountain with God (Ex. 32). They refuse to take the land God has promised (Num. 13–14).

One of the worst rebellions is led by Korah, Dathan, and Abiram. They, along with 250 chiefs, stand against Moses and Aaron, challenging their callings and their roles, saying, "'The whole community is holy, every one of them, and the LORD is with them. Why then do you set yourselves above the LORD's assembly?'" (Num. 16:3). They are envious of Moses' and Aaron's authority and question God's choice of leaders. God tells them through Moses in Exodus 19:5–6 that they are to be a "kingdom of priests and a holy nation," but this status does not negate God's appointing of persons to *shepherd*, guide, and govern them. Moses tells them that death is how they will know "'that the LORD has *sent me* to do all these things and that it was not *my idea*'" (Num. 16:28, emphasis mine). Then God kills them for challenging Moses and Aaron.

I'm sharing these examples from Moses' life to show you that even God's anointed one does not have an easy calling. He faces difficulties from outside the Hebrew people and from within the Hebrew people. However, Moses is able to persevere because the "I AM WHO I AM" is with him.

In contrast to the people, Moses is meek and faithful (Num. 12:3, 7). Even though the people grumble, Moses is compassionate. He often intercedes on their behalf, begging God to have mercy and not consume them in his anger (Ex. 32:30–32; Num. 14:13–19). The Lord speaks to Moses face-to-face, "as one speaks to a friend" (Ex. 33:11). Moses finds favor with God (vv. 12–17). Moses "sees the form of the LORD" (Num. 12:8), and is called God's servant (Ex. 14:31; Num. 12:8; Deut. 34:5). Even though Moses disobeys God at the waters of Meribah and therefore is not allowed to lead the people into the promised land (Num. 20:2–13), at the end of his life it is still said, "Since then, no prophet has risen in Israel like Moses, whom the LORD knew face to face, who did all those signs and wonders the LORD sent him to do in Egypt—to Pharaoh and to all his officials and to his whole land. For no one has ever shown the mighty power or performed the awesome deeds that Moses did in the sight of all Israel" (Deut. 34:10–12).

THE CALL OF JOSHUA

Moses' story often overshadows that of his successor Joshua, but Joshua plays an important role in the story of Israel too. Like in a relay race where one runner passes the baton to the next runner, Joshua is commissioned by God to take up Moses' calling and tasks. As Moses' successor, Joshua finishes the race Moses began by leading the people of God into the promised land and serving as their *shepherd*.

Who is Joshua, and what is he doing before his calling as shepherd? Joshua is Moses' assistant from his youth and is given a new name by Moses (Ex. 24:13; 33:11; Num. 11:28; 13:16). Joshua's call is a "developing" call. In his role as assistant and military leader, Joshua leads the Israelite army against the Amalekites and overcomes them (Ex. 17:13). On another occasion, he goes up the mountain with Moses when God gives the Ten Commandments (Ex. 24:13). Still later, when Moses leaves the Tent of Meeting, Joshua stands guard at the tent (Ex. 33:11). Joshua goes to Canaan as a spy and is one of only two spies who says they are ready to take the land God has promised (Num. 13). He is described as one who "wholly followed the LORD" (Num. 32:11–12 ESV). Joshua is upright in character and an obedient worshipper of Israel's God.

Joshua's calling is very different from Moses' calling. God calls Joshua through Moses. In Numbers 27, God takes Moses up a mountain to look into the promised land and tells Moses he will not be able to enter it. Even though Moses has a unique and personal relationship with God, he disobeyed the Lord in the Desert of Zin. As a consequence, he is not allowed to finish the job God called him to do (Deut. 32:48–52). Moses responds to this difficult reality by immediately praying for a new *shepherd* for the Hebrew people, someone who will lead them into the new land. Moses anticipates a need God had already foreseen—the need for a successor.

Moses prays, "'Let the LORD, the God of the spirits of all flesh, appoint a man over the congregation, who shall go out before them and come in before them, who shall lead them out and bring them in, that the congregation of the LORD may not be as sheep that have no shepherd'" (Num. 27:16–17 ESV).

God responds by telling Moses to "'take Joshua . . . a man in whom is the Spirit'" (Num. 27:18 ESV). God isn't caught off-guard by Moses' prayer or the need for a successor. Rather, God has already gone ahead of Moses and prepared one. We know this because the text says the Spirit is *already with* Joshua. To confirm his choice to Israel, God instructs Moses to commission Joshua in front of the assembly (Num. 27:19–23; Deut. 3:28).

How Joshua Fulfilled His Calling

God repeatedly assures Joshua that he will be with him: "'It is the LORD who goes before you. He will be with you; he will not leave you or forsake you'" (Deut. 31:8 ESV).[7] God doesn't call Joshua to a task only to abandon Joshua to do it on his own. No; once again we are reminded that this is God's call and God's task. He will see it through and will be with the one he is sending. *The presence of God accompanies the child and call of God, and this promise still holds true today.*

As we read about the materialization of Joshua's call in the book of Joshua, we find he continues in faithfulness to the Lord by doing what God commands him. He serves to protect the Israelites not only physically but also spiritually (Josh. 24), and with God's grace, he does a good job. "Israel served the LORD throughout the lifetime of Joshua" (Josh. 24:31). When it comes time for Joshua to die, the same description that was used for Moses is now used for Joshua: he is called "the servant of the LORD" (Josh. 24:29). Throughout the book of Joshua, Moses is identified as "the servant of the LORD."[8] There is no higher honor or title given to someone than "servant of the LORD."

For those who have grown up in the church, for whom there is no dramatic story of a terrible past life being made new, Joshua's story is good news. In Joshua we have someone who is faithful to God from beginning to end. Through their stories, we can see that God uses all kinds of people. He redeems and calls the outcast (Moses); he commissions and anoints those who have been faithful from youth (Joshua). Yet how these men ended in life is more important than how they began. In the end, both Moses and Joshua died as *servants of the Lord.*

THE CALL OF DAVID

Like Moses, David is a well-known individual. Because of his familiarity, we might be prone to skip right by. But I want to stop and consider David because, like Moses, he is a unique person in Old Testament salvation history. We are given many details about David's calling and commissioning that I think will be helpful to us.

David is an unlikely candidate for king of Israel (1 Sam. 16:1–13). He is, for example, the youngest of seven brothers. In our culture that may not mean much, but in a culture that values and esteems the firstborn and gives more rights to the firstborn, this *is* a big deal. David is the furthest away from the firstborn; he is the last. Yet David is awarded a greater inheritance than his brothers.

Before becoming king, David is a shepherd. He is given a lowly job among his brothers, a job that sends him far from home and sometimes into danger. When the prophet Samuel comes to anoint one of Jesse's sons as king, Jesse doesn't even bother to send for David. Only at Samuel's prompting is David brought in from the fields. David is young and doesn't have a kingly appearance. When Samuel looks at Jesse's oldest son, Eliab, Samuel thinks he must be God's chosen. But God says to Samuel, "'Do not consider his appearance or his height, for I have rejected him'" (1 Sam. 16:7a). Eliab fits Samuel's expectations, but not God's.

David is young when he is anointed as king by Samuel (1 Sam. 16:13), but he does not begin to reign until he is thirty (2 Sam. 5:4). His journey from pasture to throne is long and arduous. In our fast-paced, have-it-all-now culture, waiting is a foreign concept. Not only do we not know how to wait, but waiting and delayed fulfillment are often seen as signs of failure. David, like Moses and so many others in Scripture, teaches us something different: God is not slow in fulfilling his promises or callings. Often, it is in the process that God prepares us for what lies ahead. If we try to rush things or get ahead of God, we might find ourselves like children behind the wheel of a car: inexperienced, lacking readiness, and a danger to ourselves and others.

Even though David is young, the last born in his family, and does not have a kingly appearance, God chooses him. Why? Because God looks at the heart. "'The LORD does not look at the things people look at. People look at the outward appearance, but the LORD looks at the heart'" (1 Sam. 16:7b). While it can be inferred from earlier texts, this is the first time we are told what God looks at when he chooses someone for a divinely appointed task. From their outward appearances, we may not understand why God chooses Moses, Peter, or Paul. But here in the calling process of David, God reveals the reason to Samuel: it is because God looks at the heart. Nothing is kept secret or hidden from God.

Yet if this is the case, how could any of us be chosen? As the great sixteenth-century Reformer John Calvin once said, "Man's nature, so to speak, is a perpetual factory of idols."[9] None of our hearts on their own would pass the test. Yet what Scripture means when it says God looks at the heart is this: he looks at *how a person has received God's grace*. Is his heart like that of Pharaoh, which hardens in response to the work of God? Or is his heart like that of Abraham or Moses, tenderized in response to the work of God? The ultimate reason God calls human beings for his work at all is his limitless grace, and the person whose heart is softened by that grace is the person God is most willing to use.

The Ministry of David

David is called to a specific task to serve as shepherd and prince over Israel (2 Sam. 5:1–5; 1 Chron. 11:2). Why? "For the sake of his people" (2 Sam. 5:12). You may remember the story: Israel is tired of being ruled by judges and demands a king. As a result, God chooses Saul to be king. But Saul disobeys God. When Samuel confronts Saul, he lies and masks his disobedience as an opportunity to sacrifice to the Lord (1 Sam. 15:10–23). Thus, the Lord rejects Saul because he first rejects the word of the Lord and thereby the Lord himself.

David is appointed to take Saul's place, and he later tells Saul's daughter Michal, who is also his wife, "It was before the LORD, who chose me above your father and above all his house, to appoint me as prince over Israel, the people of the LORD'" (2 Sam. 6:21 ESV). Later, God reminds David through his prophet, Nathan, of the task to which he has called him: "'I took you from the pasture, from tending the flock, and appointed you ruler over my people Israel'" (2 Sam. 7:8).

David's calling as king means he is a military leader, protecting the people of Israel from invaders and enemies who want to destroy this rather new nation. He is also a spiritual leader who, after being anointed king over all of Israel following Saul's death, brings the ark of God to Jerusalem. David leads the procession of the ark with praise and worship to God, "leaping and dancing before the LORD" (2 Sam. 6:16). David makes offerings and blesses the people (vv. 18–19). We see here that God gives David, the spiritual leader of his people, the gift of music and prose. David is a worship leader, penning the greatest songs and prayers to God, which compose much of the book of Psalms.

David's call to serve as ruler of the people of Israel is essentially a call to *shepherding*. He goes from shepherding sheep to shepherding people (2 Sam. 24:17). He protects, leads, and feeds them. He is their physical and spiritual keeper. After bringing the ark of the covenant to Jerusalem, David wants to build God a temple in which to place the ark. The word of the Lord comes to the prophet Nathan concerning this plan and says, "Wherever I have moved with all the Israelites, did I ever say to any of their *rulers whom I commanded to shepherd my people Israel*, 'Why have you not built me a house of cedar?'" (2 Sam. 7:7, emphasis mine). In this verse God clearly articulates that those he has called to rule are shepherds of his people, which includes David. Like the calls of Moses, Joshua, and other rulers, David's call is ultimately a call to shepherd God's people.

How David Fulfilled His Calling

In keeping with the way he called Moses and Joshua, God promises his presence to David (1 Sam. 18:12, 28). "And David became greater and greater, for the LORD, the God of hosts, was *with him*" (2 Sam. 5:10 ESV, emphasis mine). Notice why David becomes greater; not because of David's own might and power but because God is with him. All the times David is in trouble and on the run from Saul, God saves David because he has appointed him. David is able to rule and unite the people of Israel only because God sees fit to do it through him. David does not need to rely on his own strength to accomplish the task God has called him to do. This would make for an impossible calling. No; God does it all, and as a result God receives the glory. "In everything he did he had great success, because the LORD was with him" (1 Sam. 18:14).

As it was with Moses and Joshua, the word of the Lord is with David. David often inquires of the Lord, and the Lord answers him.[10] Through David we have God's inspired Word written down for us. The psalms of David are also the psalms of Jesus, who often quotes from them. The last words of David are a psalm in which he recognizes his role as God's mouthpiece:

> "The Spirit of the LORD spoke through me;
>   his word was on my tongue." (2 Sam. 23:2–3a).

Like Moses' calling, however, David's calling is not an easy one. He enters into Saul's service even though he is appointed to take Saul's place. Saul tries to kill David multiple times and is David's enemy for the rest of his life (1 Sam. 18:29). Because of this, David is often on the run. He tells Jonathan, his friend and Saul's son, there "'is only a step between me and death'" (1 Sam. 20:3). David fights many battles, including the famous battle against Goliath, and doesn't have the trust of all the people. His calling isn't easy. Several times Saul unknowingly places himself at David's mercy. But instead of killing Saul, David says to his men, "'The LORD forbid that I should do such a thing to my master, the LORD's anointed, or lay my hand on him; for he is the anointed of the LORD'" (1 Sam. 24:6). David is patient and trusts and fears the Lord.

However, David also has serious moral failings. Scripture tells us he sleeps with another man's wife, Bathsheba, and then tries to cover it up. When the plan doesn't work, David gives orders to end the man's life (2 Sam. 11). After her husband's death, David takes Bathsheba as his wife. David, at the height of his ministry as king, is now at his lowest point as adulterer and murderer, and what he has done displeases the Lord (v. 27). He suffers many consequences as a result of his sin.

The fact that God calls you to ministry doesn't insulate you from temptation and sin. All of us, ministers included, can fall into serious sin if we are not careful. Perhaps some of you feel called by God but are hesitant because you feel like a past sin makes you unfit for ministry. You feel as if you've ruined your *only* chance to be used by God.

The good news we find in David's story is that once he is confronted with his sin, he repents to the Lord (unlike his predecessor, Saul, who lies and tries to offer a false sacrifice to God). David prays for God to have mercy on him and to create in him a clean heart (Psalm 51). God forgives David and continues to use him. Sisters, we serve a gracious God who stands ready to forgive all those who turn to him and repent with humble hearts.

At the end of his life, David is described as "the man exalted by the Most High, the man anointed by the God of Jacob" (2 Sam. 23:1). David's calling teaches us to not think about our calling as something that will happen in the future but rather as something that begins the moment God calls us. The trials, the preparation, the studies, and the waiting are all necessary to the call God has given us. Like David, will we be found faithful, fully trusting in the Lord and his timing?

THE CALL OF JEREMIAH

When we think about the prophets, it is hard to choose just one to consider. What I like about Jeremiah is that he shares a number of personal, firsthand accounts about his calling and his inward struggles regarding it. In Jeremiah we find someone who is open about the hardships of ministry and the temptation to just walk away, yet who is faithful despite them.

Jeremiah's calling begins before birth: "'Before I formed you in the womb I knew you, before you were born I set you apart; I appointed you as a prophet to the nations'" (Jer. 1:5). Jeremiah's appointment as a prophet is born in the mind of God long before Jeremiah is conceived. Jeremiah is created with a purpose and an appointment already in place without him knowing it. God's sovereignty over Jeremiah's birth and life is evidenced by his appointment.

It is not as if Jeremiah is unique in that his life and calling are ordered long before his birth. David also says that who we are is known to God even before our bodies have taken shape (Ps. 139:13–16). Rather, what is unique is that God chooses to *reveal* this act of sovereignty to Jeremiah. To be sure, what is true of Jeremiah is true of the other people we have discussed in this chapter and people we have yet to discuss. For example, Paul describes his call almost identically, saying, "But when God, who set me apart from my mother's womb and called me by his grace, was pleased to reveal his Son in me so that I might preach him among the Gentiles, my immediate response was not to consult any human being" (Gal. 1:15–16).

We can trust that God has had the plan of salvation laid out in his mind from the beginning. It isn't a plan he's made up on the go. Therefore, who he uses and for what purposes he uses them are part of this great plan that comes to full realization in the person of Jesus Christ. Scripture makes it clear that this plan was conceived by God before the foundation of the world: "For he chose us in him before the creation of the world to be holy and blameless in his sight" (Eph. 1:4).

What is Jeremiah doing when God calls him to become a prophet? He is serving God as a priest. You might say that Jeremiah is already a minister and God calls him to another ministry. Yet Jeremiah still feels inadequate for the task at hand. "'Alas, Sovereign LORD,'" I said, 'I do not know how to speak; I am too young'" (Jer. 1:6). Jeremiah feels unqualified for his mission, but *he doesn't need to be qualified—he only needs to be called.* God tells him he will give him the words to say (vv. 7, 9); he will lead him (vv. 7, 10); and he will be with him (v. 8). Jeremiah is to be *God's vessel for God's use and for God's glory.* The excuse that Jeremiah is too young or incapable doesn't carry any weight where God is concerned. Twentieth-century German theologian and martyr Dietrich Bonhoeffer wrote:

[The call] comes over a person from the outside, not from the longings of one's own heart; it does not rise up out of one's most unseen wishes and hopes. The word that confronts us, seizes us, takes us captive, binds us fast, does not come from the depths of our souls. It is the foreign, the unfamiliar, unexpected, forceful, overpowering word of the Lord that calls into his service whomsoever and whenever God chooses . . . And then all at once this foreign, this faraway, unfamiliar, overwhelming word becomes the incredibly familiar, incredibly near, persuading, captivating, enticing word of the Lord's love, yearning for his creature.[11]

The Ministry of Jeremiah

We know from the very beginning that Jeremiah is appointed as a prophet, but what does that entail? First, Jeremiah's calling mostly involves a ministry of the Word; he is told to "go and proclaim" (Jer. 2:2). We do not know how or in what form "the word of the LORD" (Jer. 1:4) comes to Jeremiah other than it comes and it is from God. Jeremiah is both a preacher and an evangelist. While most of his ministry is spent proclaiming God's word of warning and the necessity of repentance to the Israelites, he also speaks words of judgment to the nations.

Second, Jeremiah is a *shepherd*. Early on in his call as prophet, God commands Jeremiah to preach a word of repentance. God promises that if the people repent and turn to God, then "'I will give you shepherds after my own heart, who will feed you with knowledge and understanding'" (Jer. 3:15 ESV). Shepherds feed the sheep with "knowledge and understanding," which come by knowing the Lord and by communicating God's word. Jeremiah understands his calling to be a prophet-shepherd as evidenced in his prayer: "I have not run away from being your shepherd" (Jer. 17:16). In communicating God's truth, Jeremiah is feeding the people spiritual nourishment. But will the sheep eat this food?

Like the others we have examined in this chapter, Jeremiah ultimately fulfills his ministry because of two promises from God: his word and his presence. The call to prophesy for the Lord comes with the promise that God will be faithful to deliver his word through Jeremiah. He is God's mouthpiece. Not only is God watching over his servant, but he tells Jeremiah, "I am watching to see that my word is fulfilled" (Jer. 1:12). God makes certain his word and mission will be fulfilled through Jeremiah not only in Jeremiah's day but ultimately in Jesus Christ. Twice in the Gospel of Matthew we are told that the word of Jeremiah has been fulfilled (Matt. 2:17; 27:9).

God's word and appointment again carries with it the promise of God's presence. He tells Jeremiah, "I am with you," admonishes him not to be afraid of his enemies, and says repeatedly that he will rescue and save him (Jer. 1:8; 15:20; 1:19). Ultimately God is saying, "I will accomplish that which I am sending you to do because I am with you."

Later in the book of Jeremiah, the prophet is contrasted with false prophets not only in their message and conduct but also in their commission. Unlike Jeremiah, whom God sends, the false prophets are sent by their own flesh and will. God says of them, "I did not send these prophets, yet they have run with their message; I did not speak to them, yet they have prophesied" (Jer. 23:21). Their doom is inevitable because they act without the Lord's call and anointing.[12]

But to whom do the sheep of Israel listen? Jeremiah or the false prophets? Sadly, as we read the book of Jeremiah, we see that the sheep do not eat the food Jeremiah gives them. Instead, they reject it. Instead of repenting, they rebel. Instead of crying out to God, they try to kill God's servant (Jer. 38:1–13). Jeremiah's call is one of great hardship and pain. He is imprisoned, beaten, and almost put to death on several occasions. The people call him a liar, and they love the false prophets (Jer. 5:31).

Although Jeremiah's initial call was one of great joy, as time goes on it becomes a great burden.[13] Jeremiah describes his initial call in this way: "When your words came, I ate them; they were my *joy* and my *heart's delight*, for I bear your name, LORD God Almighty" (Jer. 15:16, emphasis mine). But then the joy is replaced by pain, and he says, "Why is my pain unending and my wound grievous and incurable? You are to me like a deceptive brook, like a spring that fails" (Jer. 15:18).

Several chapters later, after beihg beaten and placed in stocks, Jeremiah is at a breaking point. He tells the Lord he has deceived him. Jeremiah is essentially saying, "This is not what I signed up for! Why did you call me to such pain?" In Jeremiah's words, "I am ridiculed all day long; everyone mocks me . . . So the word of the LORD has brought me insult and reproach all day long" (Jer. 20:7–8).

Yet even though Jeremiah is being crushed on every side, persecuted, and mocked, *he cannot stop prophesying*; he *cannot quit* fulfilling the call that God has placed on him: "But if I say, 'I will not mention his Word or speak anymore in his name,' his Word is in my heart like a fire, a fire shut up in my bones. I am weary of holding it in; indeed, I cannot'" (Jer. 20:9). A true calling from God cannot be easily cast aside. The Spirit of God and the call is stronger than Jeremiah's pain.

WHAT CAN WE LEARN?

While our world has changed from then to today, what has not changed is the nature of God and the nature of man. If we look, we can see ourselves in these individuals—afraid, full of excuses, surprised—when God's call comes to us. We can relate to Jeremiah, who cannot stop fulfilling his call, or to Joshua, who has been faithful to the Lord since his youth and now finds himself in a position of leadership. Their stories can also comfort us regarding the nature of God. He is the God who calls people to serve on his behalf. He is the God who is with us. He is the God who goes with us and teaches us what to say. So then, what can we conclude about these individuals that relates to our own callings?

The first concluding observation is a pattern throughout the Old Testament of God raising up individuals for a task that goes beyond the call of being a child of God. They are all called by God to serve on behalf of God for the people of God by delivering the Word of God. Imitating the Great Shepherd, they are shepherds of

God's people by giving them spiritual food (the word of God) and leading them in truth. In each person's story, we see the sovereignty of God at work, whether it is God protecting Moses as an infant or telling Jeremiah he chose him before he was born. We see that God is involved in time, history, creation, and people's individual lives to bring about his kingdom.

Second, God's presence accompanies them. God never calls them to a place he does not go. Like these men, our callings won't be easy. We may endure suffering for the sake of Christ. But take heart in knowing that if God has called you to something or someplace, you will never be alone. He is with you.

Third, these men are obedient to God's call on their lives. Even though they may be unqualified, lacking in confidence, unrighteous, and weak, God chooses them, and they respond in obedience. Their testimony of faithfulness even when the calling and task are overwhelming and scary should encourage us as we face our own calls. Your ministry doesn't depend on your strengths or weaknesses but on the strengths of the One who has called you—Jesus Christ.

Fourth, all these men view themselves as humble servants of the Lord. When we obey God, we glorify God. In the end it is not about us being exalted or glorified, having a successful career, or making lots of money. It is about God receiving glory and his message of love in Jesus Christ being made known through us. The act of calling is a reminder and serves as a sign that God continues to be involved in our world and cares about people.

Last, God is calling people back to himself to establish a people for himself. The way in which he is accomplishing this purpose, Scripture tells and shows us, is by calling and raising up individuals to establish, guard, lead, feed, and shepherd a people for God.

Let's turn now to the next chapter and ask this question: *Do we see a similar pattern in how God calls and uses people in the New Testament?*

God and Father of our Lord Jesus Christ, Father of mercies and God of all comfort, dwelling on high but having regard for the lowly, knowing all things before they come to pass: We give you thanks that from the beginning you have gathered and prepared a people to be heirs of the covenant of Abraham, and have raised up prophets, kings, and priests, never leaving your temple untended. We praise you also that from the creation you have graciously accepted the ministry of those whom you have chosen.[14]

REFLECTION QUESTIONS

1. What additional observations can you make concerning the callings of Moses, Joshua, David, and Jeremiah?

2. What observations about their callings give you comfort as you think about your own calling?

3. All of these individuals faced hardships in their callings. Are you willing to suffer for the sake of the gospel? Why or why not?

DISCUSSION QUESTIONS

1. Whose calling story in the Old Testament do you identify with the most? Why?

2. When have you felt God's presence as you have pursued God's call?

3. What promises of God have carried you through difficult times?

PERSONAL EXERCISES

1. Examine your calling within the framework I suggested in the chapter: called to serve on behalf of God, for the people of God, to administer the Word of God. How does your calling fit within this grid?

2. Have you given God excuses for why you are not up to the task? If so, write them down. Are they similar to excuses Moses or Jeremiah gave God? What does Scripture have to say about our excuses?

3. Examine the callings of one or two others in the Old Testament (examples: Abraham, Samuel, Isaiah, Jonah). Write down observations like I did in this chapter. Do you come to any of the same conclusions? Can you make any new observations?

4. Read Hebrews 11. What can we learn in this chapter about the calling and vocational ministry of those people in the Old Testament?

5. Read 1 Peter 1:10–12 and 2 Peter 1:20–21. What more can we learn about the ministry of the prophets from these verses? Notice how often the Spirit is mentioned—not just the Holy Spirit but the Spirit of Christ.

MINISTRY SPOTLIGHT:

BARBARA PEMBERTON

B arbara Pemberton was raised by her grandparents in Jackson, Mississippi. They faithfully took her to church. Her grandmother, who was in charge of the nursery ministry, had a profound impact on her.

Barbara became a Christian as a child and was quickly discipled through a ministry called Discipleship Training. A woman led a group of children in memorizing Scripture and learning theology through their early teen years. About a year after she came to Christ, Barbara experienced a call to ministry. While sitting on her bed one evening, she read Isaiah 6:8: "Then I heard the voice of the Lord saying, 'Whom shall I send? And who will go for us?' And I said, 'Here am I. Send me!'"

"Tears dropped onto my Bible," Barbara said. "I said, 'Send me!' What that meant to my young heart then, and continuing on to ministry now, is I'll do whatever. It didn't necessarily mean missions or youth work or women's ministry or any of those things—although I've kind of done all of them. Every day there's something new. You never know what God has in store when you are just willing."

Barbara didn't pursue formal ministry right away. In her words, she took some detours. She earned a degree in television broadcasting, and worked in radio after graduating from college. She married and had three sons. Her husband was an engineer, and they moved quite often—all over the country and abroad.

While Barbara was serving as a youth minister in a church she and her husband helped plant in Anchorage, Alaska, God laid it on her heart to go to seminary. She knew she needed to learn more. She wanted to be able to answer young people's questions about Scripture and help fill in the gaps in their theology. The problem was, there was no evangelical seminary near their home.

She shared this desire with her husband. They were soon transferred to Texas, which allowed her to attend Southwestern Baptist Theological Seminary in Fort Worth. At Southwestern, Barbara earned a master of arts in theology/philosophy of religion. While at Southwestern, she took a class called Biblical Basis of Missions from a visiting missionary. This professor assigned the class a paper on the five pillars of Islamic orthopraxy.

God used this class to shape and change the direction of Barbara's calling: to teach Christians the truth about Islam so that they will be able to stand firm in their faith in Jesus Christ when talking to Muslims and know how to share the gospel of Jesus with them. After graduating, she attended Baylor University and earned a doctorate of philosophy in religion with a specialization in world religions. Barbara says it was very important for her to do her masters work in theology and to be firmly rooted in her Christian faith. Because of this foundation, she has never been lured away nor has her faith been shaken as she has studied other religions.

Barbara has been a professor at Ouachita Baptist University since 2002, teaching world religions and Christian discipleship. She primarily teaches world religions to students so that they will know how to better engage people of other faiths with the gospel of Jesus Christ. Barbara also directs Ouachita's Carl Goodson Honors Program and oversees the Pruet Sisterhood, a student group of young women called to gospel ministry.

Barbara never thought she would be a teacher, but she loves what she does because she is serving the Lord. When she returned to her home church after graduating from seminary, Barbara visited her discipleship leader. This woman said, "Finally, the last one has returned!" Everyone in Barbara's discipleship group had gone into ministry.

When I asked her what advice she would offer you, Barbara said, "Study! Prepare! Second Timothy 2:15 has been my life verse since I was six years old. I believe God delights in surprising us with unexpected, challenging opportunities to serve. And be joyful! It's contagious!"

CHAPTER 2

Calling in the New Testament

In chapter 1 we observed that God calls and raises up individuals to serve on his behalf for the people of God by delivering the Word of God. We concluded that God calls some people to a *shepherding* role. As we look now at the New Testament, a surprising twist occurs in the drama of calling. Just like in a movie where we learn something new about a main character that helps explain his previous actions, in the New Testament we learn something new about God that helps explain his actions in the Old Testament.

What is this twist? That God himself, in the person of his Son, Jesus Christ, has come to do what he has asked his shepherds to do in the past. God himself, in Jesus Christ, will become incarnate to be our Great Shepherd. In many ways, his calling of those Old Testament individuals was preparation for his own coming and ministry. This doesn't mean the calling of Jesus Christ to become flesh was Plan B, though. It was God's plan from the beginning!

> For he chose us *in him before the creation of the world* to be holy and blameless in his sight ... In him we were also chosen, having been predestined according to the plan of him who works out everything in conformity with the purpose of his will, in order that we, who were the first to put our hope in Christ, might be for the praise of his glory. (Eph. 1:4, 11–12, emphasis mine)
>
> The Son is the image of the invisible God, the firstborn over all creation. For in him all things were created: things in heaven

and on earth, visible and invisible, whether thrones or powers or rulers or authorities; all things have been created through him and for him. He is before all things, and in him all things hold together. (Col. 1:15–17)

Professor and preacher Robert Smith Jr. says, "This means that in the mind of God, Calvary was a forethought and not an afterthought. God did not react to the fall of Adam and Eve, but rather he pre-acted *before* the fall of Adam and Eve. The Old Testament proclaimed that Christ was coming. The New Testament announced that Christ has come and will come again."[1] The individuals in the previous chapter are preparing the way for the coming of Jesus Christ. In turn, the Son of God perfectly fulfills every role to which he has called people in the Old Testament (prophet, priest, king, and shepherd) and even goes beyond them (as the *perfect* prophet, priest, king, and shepherd). What we see in the Old Testament—God calling people to serve on his behalf to administer the Word of God for the people of God—mirrors the call he has already given himself in Jesus Christ. They serve as precursors to his coming (Heb. 1:1–4; 3:1–6; 11:13).

We therefore begin our survey of the New Testament with Jesus Christ himself, because his calling will become the calling of his disciples as well. Jesus himself said, "'As the Father has sent me, I am sending you'" (John 20:21). Jesus Christ is the lens through which we are to view and understand God calling and sending individuals in all of Scripture as well as the lens through which to view our own callings! In this chapter we will look at the call of Jesus Christ as well as the call of two of his disciples, Peter and Paul, and finally of Timothy. In their callings, we will see some continuity with the Old Testament. At the same time, there will be discontinuity. For while the people of the Old Testament are looking to the future and what God will accomplish, the people of the New Testament are looking back to the cross and resurrection, to what God has already accomplished.

What We Can Learn from the Calling of Jesus

In John's Gospel, Jesus continually refers to the Father as the One who sends him and refers to himself as the one who is sent.[2] Look at the endnote and see how many times Jesus talks about being sent by the Father. Being sent is central to Jesus' identity. Jesus says the Father, in sending him, testifies concerning himself, and Jesus testifies concerning the Father: "'For the works that the Father has given me to finish—the very works that I am doing—*testify that the Father has sent me. And the Father who sent me* has himself testified concerning me'" (John 5:36–37, emphasis mine). Since they share the same nature— the nature of God—they are testifying to the world about each other. This is why Jesus can say, "Anyone who has seen me has seen the Father'" (John 14:9).[3] This testimony is made possible because the Father sends the Son, and the Son "made himself nothing by taking the very nature of a servant, being made in human likeness. And being found in appearance as a man, he humbled himself by becoming obedient to death—even death on a cross!" (Phil. 2:7–8).

At this point you may be wondering if being sent by God is the same thing as being called by God. Let's pause and think back to the previous chapter. In regard to Moses' call, God doesn't use the word *call*, but the words *go* and *send*. He says, "'So now, *go*. I am *sending* you to Pharaoh to bring my people the Israelites out of Egypt'" (Ex. 3:10, emphasis mine). For Joshua, the word that comes from God through Moses is this: "'Be strong and courageous, for you must *go* with this people into the land that the LORD swore to their ancestors to give them, and you must divide it among them as their inheritance. The LORD himself *goes* before you and will be with you; he will never leave you nor forsake you'" (Deut. 31:7–8, emphasis mine). To Jeremiah God says, "'You must *go* to everyone I *send* you to and say whatever I command you'" (Jer. 1:7). Remember not to get hung up on terminology. Scripture uses different terms to describe the same reality—God calling individuals to *do* something. God's call is never stationary.

How Jesus Fulfilled His Calling

Do you remember the promises that accompanied the callings of those individuals we examined in the previous chapter? They were promised the presence of God and the word of God. Jesus, who is the Son of God, God incarnate, testifies that the Father is with him. Even Jesus, the Son of God, is promised the presence of God in his being sent. "'The one who sent me is *with me*; he has not left me alone, for I always do what pleases him'" (John 8:29, emphasis mine). We also see the Spirit of God ministering to the Son of God at his baptism (Luke 3:21–22) and throughout his ministry (Luke 4:14).[4] Peter testifies, "God anointed Jesus of Nazareth with the *Holy Spirit* and power" (Acts 10:38, emphasis mine). Finally, the Holy Spirit raises Jesus from the dead (Rom. 8:11). Then—get this—Jesus turns around and promises the Holy Spirit to all who believe and to all he is sending (John 16:7; 17:15–27; 20:21–22)!

Jesus is also promised God's word. He says, "'For I did not speak on my own, but *the Father who sent me commanded me to say all that I have spoken'*" (John 12:49, emphasis mine). The irony here is that John tells us that Jesus *is* the Word of God made flesh (John 1)! Don't miss this. Jesus embodies—in fact *is the incarnation of*—these promises!

And guess what Jesus promises his disciples as he is sending them. He promises to send them the Holy Spirit, who will tell them what to say! As he commissions the Twelve in Matthew's Gospel, Jesus tells them, "'But when they arrest you, do not worry about what to say or how to say it. At that time you will be given what to say, for it will not be you speaking, but the Spirit of your Father speaking through you'" (Matt. 10:19–20).

So as we enter into the New Testament, what has changed? God himself has come! He has sent the Son to reconcile the world through himself as the perfect prophet, who is also the Word of God; the perfect priest, who is also the Lamb who was slain; and the perfect king, who is also the Good Shepherd.[5] After his resurrection, the One who is sent does the sending. "Again Jesus said, 'Peace be with you! *As the Father has sent me, I am sending you.'* And with that he breathed on them and said, 'Receive the Holy Spirit'" (John 20:21–22, emphasis mine).

As we turn our attention to Peter, Paul, and Timothy, we are faced with the question, does the pattern from the Old Testament still continue? Now that Jesus has come, does God still call individuals to ministry like he did in the past? As we consider this, let us remember that the Father, Son, and Holy Spirit are sending us to do the work of ministry.

> Then Jesus came to them and said, "All authority in heaven and on earth has been given to me. Therefore go and make disciples of all nations, baptizing them in the name of the Father and of the Son and of the Holy Spirit, and teaching them to obey everything I have commanded you. And surely I am with you always, to the very end of the age." (Matt. 28:18–20)

THE CALL OF PETER

Peter is probably the most well-known of Jesus' twelve disciples. He is the most outspoken disciple in the Gospels, and is in Jesus' inner circle of three with James and John. I want to consider Peter's calling because I believe it will help us as we consider our own callings.

Peter, like his brother Andrew, is a fisherman when Jesus calls him. He is uneducated according to rabbinic standards of the period. Peter is "ordinary" (Acts 4:13). From a worldly perspective, Peter isn't special, yet Jesus chooses him and his brother, saying, "'Follow Me, and I will make you fishers of men'" (Matt. 4:19 NKJV). Even though Jesus calls many disciples, he sets apart Peter and eleven other men for a unique relationship with him. Eventually Jesus sends them out to minister the way he has taught them: preaching the kingdom of God, healing the sick, raising the dead, casting out demons, and cleansing lepers (Matt. 10:1–20). The twelve disciples receive a unique call that, while overlapping with the call of other disciples (i.e., the call to share the gospel), is nevertheless special to them. Their testimony and explanation of the death and resurrection of

Jesus Christ will become authoritative in the church. In fact, it is their *written* testimony that will become the New Testament. Peter's testimony is captured in the Gospels, the book of Acts, and the two letters he wrote, 1 and 2 Peter.

The Ministry of Peter

Peter's commission involves more than that of the other eleven disciples. When Jesus calls his first disciples in Luke 5:1–11, the Gospel writer focuses particularly on Peter. Even though James and John are present, and they also drop everything to follow Jesus, he addresses Peter. "'Don't be afraid,' Jesus says to him, 'from now on you will fish for people'" (v. 10). Later in Jesus' ministry, he tells Peter:

> And I tell you, you are Peter, and on this rock I will build my church, and the gates of hell shall not prevail against it. I will give you the keys of the kingdom of heaven, and whatever you bind on earth shall be bound in heaven, and whatever you loose on earth shall be loosed in heaven. (Matt. 16:18–19 ESV)

Some interpret this text as Jesus saying he will build his church on Peter. Others interpret it as Jesus saying he will build his church on Peter's confession, given just a few verses prior. Jesus asks his disciples, "'Who do you say I am?' Peter responds, 'You are the Messiah, the Son of the living God'" (vv. 15–16). Whatever the precise interpretation of the text above, it is clear that Peter will have an important role in the establishment of the church, which is founded on the confession of Jesus as both the Messiah and Son of God.

After Jesus' resurrection, just before he ascends into heaven, Jesus commands Peter to care for his sheep. Likewise, our callings are nothing other than commands of God. A call isn't God asking if we would consider doing something for him or him pleading with us. Rather, it is a *divine directive* to do something. Jesus tells Peter three times in John 21:15–17 (ESV) to take care of his sheep: "'Feed my lambs,'" he says. "'Tend my sheep.'" And finally, "'Feed my sheep.'" Jesus is calling Peter to *shepherd* his sheep. Peter is to do this not just because Jesus is telling him to do so, but because he loves Jesus. He shows his love for Jesus by doing what Jesus commands him! "'Do you love me?'" Jesus asks Peter. Love of God, which stems from being loved *by* God, is the motivation to shepherd Jesus' sheep. Who are his sheep? They are his people, the ones for whom Jesus died just days prior.

How will Peter feed Jesus' sheep? Just like we read in Jeremiah, people are fed with the Word of God. Shortly after Jesus' ascension and the coming of the Holy Spirit in Acts 2, Peter "feeds" people by preaching a powerful evangelistic sermon. Peter's ministry of the Word is his highest calling. He explains to the gentiles in Acts 10:42, "[Jesus] commanded us to preach to the people and to testify that he is the one whom God appointed as judge of the living and the dead."

In Acts 6, seven men are chosen to serve the widows and the poor because it isn't right that Peter and the other eleven apostles "should give up preaching the word of God to serve tables" (v. 2 ESV). This verse should not be read as if Peter is above serving the poor; rather, Peter is saying that to give up his calling would be to disobey the One who has called him. As one of the Twelve, he is to communicate what Jesus has communicated to him. As we continue reading the book of Acts, Peter does indeed minister to the physical needs of some by healing the sick (Acts 3:1–8; 9:32–43), but he never does these things at the expense of his primary calling to preach the gospel.

Many of us will be tempted to say "yes" to every ministry opportunity that comes our way. God may have called you to ministry, but he hasn't called you to *every* ministry. Peter's story teaches us that we must be careful not to get involved in every type of ministry available, especially if it will prevent or distract us from the *kind of ministry* God has called us to do. If we do this, we disobey God.

How Peter Fulfilled His Ministry

Like the other people we've looked at, Peter is able to fulfill his calling because God is with him in the person of the Holy Spirit. Just before his ascension, Jesus says to the Twelve, "But you will receive power when the Holy Spirit comes on you; and you will be my witnesses in Jerusalem, and in all Judea and Samaria, and to the ends of the earth" (Acts 1:8). The Holy Spirit's coming fulfills Jesus' promise that he will not leave them as orphans (John 14:16–18). As we read Acts, we find that the Holy Spirit and the word of God accompany Peter and his ministry (Acts 4:31; 10:9–48).

Peter, to whom Jesus once had said, "'Get behind me, Satan!'" (Matt. 16:23), is the same person Jesus has now established as shepherd of his people, the church. The same Peter who once denied Jesus three times (Matt. 26:30–35, 69–75; Luke 22:31–34, 54–62) is now being used by Jesus to proclaim his death and resurrection.

For someone like me, who messes up frequently, Peter's story, like David's and others', reminds me of the grace and loving-kindness of our God, who never tires of giving us another chance and uses us despite our unworthiness.

THE CALL OF PAUL

Just like Moses, Paul seems at first glance like an unlikely individual, but God uses him mightily in apostolic ministry. Paul's story is special, and therefore has much to teach us about vocational ministry. With prayerful anticipation, let's now turn to Paul.

Paul, like Moses, has a supernatural, one-of-a-kind encounter with Jesus Christ. In fact, Paul is the most unlikely of people to become a follower of Christ. Why? For one thing, Paul was a highly ranked Pharisee. In his own words, he tells the churches in Galatia, "I was advancing in Judaism beyond many of my own age among my people and was extremely zealous for the traditions of my fathers" (Gal. 1:14). Even more importantly, Paul persecuted and killed Christians because he believed Jesus was accursed and a false prophet. Paul is not very different from a contemporary religious fanatic who is willing to kill for his faith. He says, "For you have heard of my former life in Judaism, how I persecuted the church of God violently and tried to destroy it" (Gal. 1:13 ESV).

In a very moving narrative of Stephen defending his faith in Jesus and being stoned to death for it, Luke tells us that one man in particular is there: Saul. "At this they covered their ears and, yelling at the top of their voices, they all rushed at [Stephen], dragged him out of the city and began to stone him. Meanwhile, the witnesses laid their coats at the feet of a young man named Saul . . . And Saul approved of their killing him" (Acts 7:57–58; 8:1).

This is the same Saul (later called Paul), the one who is "still breathing out murderous threats against the Lord's disciples" (Acts 9:1), who heads to Damascus to take followers of Jesus "as prisoners to Jerusalem" (v. 2), and whom Jesus meets and calls, Paul's story is a testimony that Jesus can take the worst of sinners and call them into relationship with him and into ministry. Paul is proof that no one is out of Jesus' reach.

Paul views his calling through the lens of God's sovereignty. Like Jeremiah, Paul begins his calling story in the letter to the Galatians with, "But when he who had set me apart before I was born . . ." (1:15 ESV). He doesn't begin his story with the encounter on the road. Rather, he prefaces it with an understanding that Jesus chose him *before* the Damascus road—in fact, he was chosen before his birth.

Paul begins his letter to Timothy by saying, "Paul, an apostle of Christ Jesus by the *will* of God" (2 Tim. 1:1 ESV, emphasis mine). Paul recognizes that his change of heart and mission are solely because God determined it. By using the words *appointed, set apart, called, commissioned,* and *assigned* to describe his calling throughout his epistles, Paul recognizes that what happened prior to and on the road to Damascus was a one-sided, God-ordained event. God, out of his grace and love, chose Paul.

The Ministry of Paul

The picture we get from Acts is that because God chose Paul, Paul cannot stop preaching! This is because his calling doesn't come from within him; the call comes from God. Because of this, God changes Paul's heart, causing him to desire his calling. Paul says, "For when I preach the gospel, I cannot boast, since I am *compelled* to preach. Woe to me if I do not preach the gospel! If I preach voluntarily, I have a reward; if not voluntarily, I am simply discharging the trust committed to me" (1 Cor. 9:16–17, emphasis mine).

When Paul meets Jesus on the road to Damascus, it is both a call to discipleship (come follow me) and a call to ministry (go and preach) (Acts 22:14–16; 26:15–18). Paul's faith event coincides with his call to ministry. This still happens today, albeit not to everyone. My husband, for example, became a Christian later in life and felt a call to preach almost simultaneously.

Paul is called to a ministry of the gospel for the building up of the people of God. In Acts 9, Jesus speaks to a disciple named Ananias in a vision and says, concerning Paul, "'This man is my chosen instrument to proclaim my name to the Gentiles and their kings and to the people of Israel'" (Acts 9:15). Paul describes his call to the Christians in Colossae this way: "I have become [the church's] servant by the commission God gave me to present to you the word of God in its fullness" (Col. 1:25). So what did Paul's ministry of the gospel look like? What form did it take? Today we have, for the most part, neatly categorized callings into specific roles and jobs. For many, if someone is called to be a pastor, they will remain a pastor of a church for the rest of their lives. But Paul's ministry takes many different forms. He is an evangelist, preacher, church planter, missionary, pastor/elder, and teacher. Most importantly, he is an apostle, one who has seen the risen Lord and who is called to establish his church.

Paul is most often called a missionary to the gentiles, which he is (Gal. 1:16); but he also preaches to and ministers among the Jews. Notice his calling in Acts 9:15 is both to the gentiles and the people of Israel. His letter to the Romans is addressed to both Jewish and gentile Christians. Paul has a far-reaching ministry. He is not defined by a title or a role; rather, he is called to be a minister of the gospel.

How Paul Viewed His Ministry

Paul views his calling through the lens of servanthood. Although Paul is one whom Jesus meets in person to call to a ministry of the gospel, and even though he is an apostle, he regards himself as a "servant of Jesus." When he speaks to the Ephesian elders in Acts 20, he says about his ministry, "However, I consider my life worth nothing to me; my only aim is to finish the race and complete the task the Lord Jesus has given me—the task of testifying to the good news of God's grace" (v. 24).

In his letter to the Corinthians, addressing divisions in the church based on leadership, Paul writes, "What, after all, is Apollos? And what is Paul? Only *servants*, through whom you came to believe—as the Lord has assigned to each his task" (1 Cor. 3:5, emphasis mine). A few verses later he refers to himself and Apollos as simply *co-workers*. Further on in the letter, Paul calls himself and Apollos "*servants* of Christ and as those entrusted with the mysteries God has revealed" (4:1, emphasis mine). The phrase "those entrusted with" is the translation of one Greek word, *oikonomous*. Another way to translate this word within its context is "administrator" or "steward."[6] Paul as an apostle is both a servant and administrator, or steward, of the mysteries of God as revealed in Jesus Christ.

In a subsequent letter to the Corinthians, Paul says, "We are therefore Christ's *ambassadors*, as though God were making his appeal through us" (2 Cor. 5:20, emphasis mine). In 1 Timothy, Paul writes to a young Timothy, saying he is thankful God has appointed Paul to "his service" (1:12). Paul also describes the church as his "workmanship" (1 Cor. 9:1 ESV), which implies he views himself as a worker of the Lord. Paul even refers to others with whom he is laboring side by side as fellow servants (Col. 1:7). Paul's understanding of his call through the lens of servanthood is in keeping with what we find with Moses and Joshua, who, though they were leaders, were called servants of the Lord.

Ministry in the West today can bring with it the temptations of fame and money. But Paul, like Jesus, teaches to view ministry from the posture of kneeling as a servant.

THE CALL OF TIMOTHY

Timothy plays an important role in Paul's ministry, and Paul writes him two letters, which are part of the New Testament. Who is Timothy, though, and what is his calling story?

The first time we hear of Timothy is when Paul comes to Lystra in Acts 16:1. Luke, the author of the book of Acts, tells us that Timothy is a disciple of Jesus Christ. His mother is a Jew, and his father is a Greek. Although his father is probably not a Christian, Timothy comes to a "sincere faith" (2 Tim. 1:5) because of the influence of his grandmother, Lois, and mother, Eunice, who have taught him the Word of God from childhood (3:14). Luke tells us Timothy has a good reputation among the believers in Lystra and in another town, Iconium, and Paul wants Timothy to accompany him on his missionary journey (Acts 16:3).

Why does Paul choose Timothy? Scripture does not give us a reason, but we can surmise Paul sees God at work in Timothy. We learn later in Paul's first letter to Timothy that prophecies have been made about Timothy (1 Tim. 1:18). Even though we do not know the content of these prophecies or when they were given, Paul refers to them within the context of Timothy's ministerial role in Ephesus. At some point, perhaps in Lystra before Paul takes Timothy with him, Paul ordains him for ministry by laying his hands on Timothy (2 Tim. 1:6). Here we have another example of God calling an individual to ministry through another believer within the context of the church, similar to the way he called Joshua through Moses.[7]

The Ministry of Timothy

Paul brings Timothy along to assist him in ministry, but we must be careful not to think of Timothy as an assistant in the way we understand assistants on church staffs today. Timothy functions as a co-minister, and Paul trusts him so much that he often sends Timothy as his representative to oversee the work of ministry in various places. At the least, we know that Timothy goes to Macedonia (Acts 19:22), Corinth (1 Cor. 4:17), Thessalonica (1 Thess. 3:2, 6), and Ephesus (1 Tim. 1:3) on Paul's behalf, and we are told in Philippians 2:19 that Paul wants to send him to Philippi as well. While Timothy is in Ephesus, Paul writes him two letters charging him to put a stop to false teachings and instead put into practice Paul's instructions for the church.

Timothy has a ministry of the Word of God for the people of God. He preaches (2 Cor. 1:19) and spreads the gospel (1 Thess. 3:2). Paul charges Timothy to "preach the word" and "correct, rebuke and encourage—with great patience and careful instruction" (2 Tim. 4:2). A few verses later, Paul tells him to "do the work of an evangelist, discharge all the duties of your ministry" (v. 5). Timothy is Paul's "co-worker" (Rom. 16:21) and "my son whom I love" (1 Cor. 4:17). Six of Paul's letters are sent from both Paul and Timothy (2 Corinthians, Philippians, Colossians, 1 Thessalonians, 2 Thessalonians, and Philemon). As we can see, Timothy plays a vital role in the establishing of the church and the spreading of the gospel of Jesus Christ.

How Timothy Fulfilled His Ministry

Several times Paul encourages Timothy to fulfill his ministry. How so? First, Paul reminds Timothy of the power of the Holy Spirit living in him (2 Tim. 1:6–14). "The power of God" is what will enable Timothy to share "in suffering for the gospel" (v. 8). This is the same power of God that saves and calls him (v. 9). God is the one who guards "the good deposit," which is the gospel, "with the help of the Holy Spirit who lives in us" (v. 14). Timothy by himself can do nothing; it is the Holy Spirit—the power of the living God—at work in his life who enables Timothy to fulfill his ministry. Scholar Philip H. Towner writes, "It is God himself who ensures the success of his mission."[8] Once again, we are reminded that it is not up to us to fulfill our ministry. If God has called us, he will see it through.

Second, Paul reminds Timothy that staying connected to and immersed in God's Word is essential to having a ministry of the Word:

> But as for you, continue in what you have learned and have become convinced of, because you know those from whom you learned it, and how from infancy you have known the Holy Scriptures, which are able to make you wise for salvation through faith in Christ Jesus. All Scripture is God-breathed and is useful

for teaching, rebuking, correcting and training in righteousness,
so that the servant of God may be thoroughly equipped for every
good work. (2 Tim. 3:14–17)

Towner says, "False teaching cannot deliver the promise of salvation."[9] Perhaps this is why Paul's command to continue in the learning of Scripture comes *before* his other command to Timothy to preach, exhort, and teach (2 Tim. 4:2).

WHAT CAN WE LEARN?

What lessons can we learn from the ministries of Jesus, Peter, Paul, and Timothy?

First, our God is a sending God. Before he called any of us in human history, he called himself. Therefore, we should view the callings of those in Scripture and our own callings through the lens of Jesus' call and ministry. If you've read or watched *The Lord of the Rings*, then you will know that Gondor was a realm in Tolkien's Middle-earth. In the absence of a king, a steward served in his place. The steward was meant to serve in the king's absence but not to sit in the king's rightful place. The seal of the stewards included initials that stood for "Servants of the King." As ministers of the gospel, we are to steward the people of God in the King's absence and prepare for his return. Just as the disciples are sent out by Jesus and imitate him in their ministry, we are being sent by Jesus and called to imitate him in our ministries.

Second, God's love is our motivation to love and shepherd his sheep. When the gospel of Jesus Christ—that he left his throne in heaven and became human to die for our sin and rise from the dead that we might be reconciled to God—takes hold of our hearts, we are utterly compelled. Our callings are lived out within the context of being loved by God and therefore loving God and loving others.

Third, the callings of Peter, Paul, and Timothy are one-sided events. God, out of his great mercy, chooses them to serve him in the establishment of the first church. Peter is just an ordinary fisherman when Jesus calls him. Paul is a terrorist on his way to persecute more Christians when Jesus stops him in his tracks and turns his life around. Timothy is serving faithfully in the church when God, through Paul, calls him to become a missionary. Our callings today are still one-sided, mercy-driven events. Why would God call someone like me or you for his kingdom work? Only because God, out of his great love and mercy, determines it will be so.

Fourth, we see in Paul's story that his calling puts tremendous pressure on him. I imagine the same can be said for Peter and Timothy. We should not think of this pressure negatively. Paul is so utterly compelled by the gospel that he could not stop preaching even if he wanted to! There have been times in my adult life when my calling was not materializing as quickly or in the way I had imagined. Discouraged, I told my husband that maybe I was mistaken about my call and should pursue a job that had nothing to do with the church or a ministry of the gospel. But even in those times of resistance and temptation to walk away, I couldn't. In those very moments, the pressure of my call was the strongest. It burned like fire in my bones, and I knew that to walk away from my call would be to disobey God.

Fifth, Peter, Paul, and Timothy viewed themselves as humble servants of the Lord. Paul often uses the word *servant* to describe himself. Shepherding people does not mean taking on the role of a CEO, lord, or king. Rather, as Jesus himself teaches by example when he washes the disciples' feet, we are to serve one another. He says, "'Very truly I tell you, no servant is greater than his master, nor is a messenger greater than the one who sent him'" (John 13:16). In Ephesians 3:8, Paul says that even though he's been called in this way, he is the least of the least: *"Although I am less than the least of all the Lord's people*, this grace was given me: to preach to the Gentiles the boundless riches of Christ" (emphasis mine). When we obey God, we glorify God, because in the end it is not about us receiving glory. It is about God receiving glory and about his message of love in Jesus Christ being made known.

As we consider our own callings in light of these individuals who are called to give themselves to the Lord, to represent him to the people, and to administer the word of God, let us remember that we cannot do it on our own. For just as the Father sent the Son, the Son in turn sends us. Therefore, the God who is calling and sending us will see it through, for he is with us. Thanks be to God!

Now may the God of peace, who through the blood of the eternal covenant brought back from the dead our Lord Jesus, that great Shepherd of the sheep, equip you with everything good for doing his will, and may he work in us what is pleasing to him, through Jesus Christ, to whom be glory for ever and ever. Amen. (Heb. 13:20–21)

REFLECTION QUESTIONS

1. What other observations can you make concerning the calling of the disciples, in particular Peter and Paul?

2. Are your observations about these individuals consistent with what we found about people in the Old Testament? If so, how? If not, why?

3. What parts of the discussions about Jesus, Peter, Paul, and Timothy were helpful?

DISCUSSION QUESTIONS

1. Whose calling story in the New Testament do you identify with most?

2. What might it look like for me to shepherd God's people?

3. What promises of God have carried you through difficult times?

4. Have you ever doubted your call? If so, what Scripture passages helped you confront these doubts?

PERSONAL EXERCISES

1. Reread and reevaluate the individuals in chapter 1 in light of Jesus' calling. How did they serve as precursors to Jesus' ministry, and how did Jesus surpass them in every role?

2. Write down all the descriptions Paul uses of himself (i.e., servant, co-worker). What do these descriptions teach us about how we are to view ministry?

3. Examine your calling again in light of chapters 1 and 2. How has our exploration of the New Testament strengthened, affirmed, or deepened your understanding of your calling?

4. Spend time in prayer for yourself as you continue to discern and obey God's calling. If you are having doubts, pray that God will continue to confirm his calling or will lead you clearly in a different direction.

MINISTRY SPOTLIGHT:

COKIESHA BAILEY ROBINSON

Cokiesha Bailey Robinson felt a call to ministry in the late 1990s when she was a student at Fisk University in Nashville, Tennessee. She was pursuing a degree in English with an emphasis in mass communications and serving as president of the Baptist Student Union. At that time, she did not see herself as a ministerial leader, but she enjoyed and was passionate about leading students spiritually.

With the hopes of becoming a journalist after many years of volunteering and working in radio and newspaper, she couldn't imagine God interrupting her plans and directing her to gospel proclamation ministry, for which she did not feel prepared or qualified. As a shy woman, Cokiesha enjoyed being on the sidelines, not being in front of people. "I couldn't see this shift coming, but he was preparing me for it all along," she said. "I'm so glad God always knows what he is doing."

After acknowledging the call, Cokiesha knew that entering seminary and surrounding herself with mentors in ministry was the next step. In 2003, she moved to Beeson Divinity School in Alabama and was licensed as a minister at her church. While at Beeson, she received the "Those Preaching Women" scholarship and was amazed at how God continued to affirm her call through other people.

While in seminary, Cokiesha interned at the historical Sixth Avenue Baptist Church in Birmingham, Alabama, under then-pastor A. B. Sutton. After marrying Timothy Robinson, whom she met while in seminary, she took a position as assistant pastor of Mount Neboh Baptist Church in New York, New York. In 2010, while serving at Mount Neboh, Cokiesha was ordained to ministry. A few years after serving in New York, she accepted a position as Director of Growth at Concord Church in Dallas, the church her father, the late E. K. Bailey, founded. In this role, she developed mentors and leaders and shaped ministries such as baptism, new members, the writing team, and the assimilation team. She was also given more preaching opportunities.

"Ultimately, each stop in my journey played a role in preparing me for the call of an evangelist, to which I would ultimately surrender to in 2014 in a full-time capacity," Cokiesha said.

In 2015, Cokiesha took a step of faith and founded Cross Spring Ministries, a full-time ministry of itinerate preaching, teaching, consulting, and mentoring women in ministry. Her commitment is to present the living water of the gospel through conference speaking, global ministry engagements, teaching, and mentoring, and to provide physical water to communities in need. In 2016 she partnered with the Rollings Foundation in South Africa to provide a water well for a community of two hundred people, and in 2017 Cokiesha provided assistance to the people of Flint, Michigan, who have been affected by toxic water.

"Our ultimate mission at Cross Spring is to play a part in lifting up the gospel of Jesus in a world and culture that is often presenting a Christ-less and cross-less gospel," she said. "We are committed to finding ways to live out the Great Commission and to put feet on the theology that we believe."

Since founding Cross Spring, Cokiesha has spoken and preached at numerous national and international conferences, churches, seminaries, and colleges. When I asked her what advice she would give you, Cokiesha said, "God doesn't call the qualified. He qualifies the called. Know that it is okay to feel overwhelmed by the call. God grants on-the-job training, and he didn't make a mistake in calling you. Also, give yourself to the journey. Be fluid and flexible. Don't despise the waiting room or jump out before it's time. We can never rush God, and there are consequences to moving ahead of him. Trust his timing."

CHAPTER 3

The Calling of Women in the Old Testament

In the last two chapters we asked these questions: *What is a call to gospel ministry? How has God called people to gospel work in the past?* and *What can we discern about a call to gospel ministry?* We looked at a handful of people from both the Old and New Testaments to see if we could observe any patterns about calling. What we found is that God indeed raises up and sets apart individuals for tasks within the people of God, namely imparting the word of God and shepherding God's people. God chooses to use sinful vessels like us for holy purposes to shepherd the church.

Now that we have seen how God calls people for service in his church and for his Word, we want to turn our attention to the next question: *Does God call women to gospel ministry?* No doubt we know God calls both men and women to a relationship with himself, and the Great Commission is for both men and women. I am confident you believe women are to be involved in the work of the church, at the very least at a volunteer level.

But if you are reading this book, it probably means you feel called to something more than volunteering in a ministry at your church—you want to give your life to gospel ministry; you feel called to make it your vocation. However, depending on the church in which you grew up, you may not be sure if this is even a possibility for you as a woman, that is, a possibility supported by Scripture or a realistic possibility (meaning few jobs in ministry may be available for women).

However, many women in the church and parachurch *are* engaged in gospel ministry today. I am introducing you to only a few in this book. In fact, women in ministry is not new. God has been using women in gospel ministry for centuries.[1]

Unfortunately, the gender wars in the evangelical church in the twentieth century (which occurred in part because of the rise of feminism) have obscured positive biblical passages in favor of women in vocational ministry. In some circles, there is so much emphasis on what women *cannot* do that positive texts have consequently been overlooked. This is why, in this chapter and the next, we will focus on the first aspect—biblical accounts of women called by God and involved in God's work. This chapter looks at women in the Old Testament, and the following chapter looks at women in the New Testament. The question we want to answer is this: Does God in Scripture call women to gospel ministry?

Usually the first text that comes to mind is 1 Timothy 2:11–15, which discusses women being silent in church, and for many this text alone is proof that women have no place in the vocational world of gospel ministry—it is a man's vocation, they say. We will discuss this text in chapter 5. We want to be faithful biblical interpreters; that is, we do not want to do anything that contradicts Scripture. So my guess is this is where many of you are stuck: you feel called by God, but when you read certain parts of Scripture, you don't see much support (if any!) for women in ministry. A tension exists between what you sense God is doing in your life and what you see in sections of Scripture.

Let me present at the outset what we *won't* find in Scripture: a case for women in full-time ministry in the way we understand full-time ministry today. In fact, we won't even find a case for *men* in full-time ministry the way we understand full-time ministry today in North America. For one thing, church in the twenty-first-century West is much different from the church we find in Scripture. Remember that the New Testament period spans only about sixty years. Acts and the Epistles tell us about the very first churches and the beginning of Christianity. Much has changed. This means that in Scripture you will not find search committees, job postings, salaries and health benefits, a large church staff, missions agencies, large church buildings and campuses, Christian publishing companies, and other parachurch organizations. The Christian world is much larger and in many ways very different from what we find in the Epistles.

Second, in biblical times, women did not have many of the rights we take for granted today. The Ancient Near Eastern (ANE) societies, of which Israel of the Bible was one, were patriarchal, meaning they were ruled by and in unbalanced favor of men. Implications of living in these societies were that women were under either their fathers' or husbands' authority; a woman's role was to care for her home; marriage was not an equal partnership; women did not have the right to initiate a divorce, nor did they necessarily receive anything if their husbands divorced them; women could not often inherit property; and women were seen as poor leaders.[2] Jewish women were not allowed to be disciples, and they were restricted from certain areas of the temple and synagogues. While they were allowed to listen, they were largely forbidden to sit at the feet of a rabbi (a posture of a disciple).[3]

Finally, even though the Bible is a story of calling, it is not a modern calling textbook or guidebook. (That's what this book is for!) We must have realistic expectations when we come to Scripture. At the same time, we must understand that submission to the authority of Scripture includes recognition of and an attempt to understand the culture in which the Bible was originally given. In light of this background, we begin by exploring women in the Old Testament God used to administer his word to his people.

THE CALL OF DEBORAH

One of the most well-known women in the Old Testament within our topic, and perhaps in all of Scripture, is Deborah. For a refresher, stop and read Judges 4:1–5:31. These passages of Scripture are interesting for several reasons. First, the same story is described in two different genres: narrative and poetry. We do not see this elsewhere in the book of Judges, although we find an interestingly similar pattern in Exodus 15 with Moses and Miriam (vv. 1–21). Second, and most striking, is Deborah herself. She is the only female judge listed in Judges and *one of only two* prophetic judges mentioned in the Old Testament (the other is Samuel). More than likely, the original hearers and readers are not expecting a woman leader for Israel.

Let's begin by setting the historical context. The Israelites disobey God, and because of their disobedience, God sells them into the hands of a foreign ruler. This is the pattern seen throughout all of Judges (2:16–19). The people disobey God; the people are sold into the hands of an oppressive ruler; the people cry out to God; God raises a person to rescue the people. The oppressive ruler in chapter 4 of Judges is Jabin, king of Canaan, and his army general is Sisera.

The Ministry of Deborah

Given the pattern already set for us in Judges 2 and 3, the expectation is that God is going to raise up a leader for Israel, specifically a judge like he does in chapter 3 with judges Othniel, Ehud, and Shamgar—all male leaders. But we are in for a surprise, a surprise that the author of Judges underlines, when Deborah is introduced. The Hebrew is emphatic: the one God has raised up is a *woman* prophet.[4] Old Testament scholar Trent C. Butler says, "This emphasis on the character's gender and multiple offices turns the reader's world upside down. The hope for Israel lies not in a man Yahweh calls specifically for the situation, but in a female judge and prophet. This turn of events might not seem so radical to you and me today, but it would have seemed unthinkable to the Israelites of the time."[5]

Scripture does not give us a "calling" story for Deborah like it does with other individuals we have studied thus far. But even though we do not know the way God calls Deborah, we do know God has appointed her to this role.

Three nouns are given to describe Deborah: woman, prophet, and wife. The first noun emphasizes her gender, the second her calling, and the third her fulfillment of societal expectations. Perhaps the mention of her husband is also meant to identify who she is, much like a last name helps identify us today. These nouns are then followed by a participle of action—she is *judging*.[6] This role of judge is reminiscent of Moses, who settled disputes among the people (Ex. 18:13). Deborah has been judging and prophesying for some time when we meet her, but the story narrows in on her role in overturning Jabin and Sisera, thereby freeing Israel from Canaan's rule.

If you go back and read the rest of Judges, you'll notice a pattern. When the people cry to the Lord, God raises up a mighty warrior to serve as judge. This kind of judge is not the same kind of judge as Deborah (Judg. 4:4–5). These judges serve more as generals and rescue the people out of the hands of their oppressors. Original hearers and readers of this text might have asked themselves, "Is Deborah going to be *this* kind of judge? *Who* is going to rescue the people?"

The text then says that Deborah calls for Barak.[7] There is an emphasis on her initiative. When Barak comes, she gives him his commissioning orders. Old Testament scholar Lawson Younger writes, "Deborah stands as God's envoy, the means by which God issues his call to Barak."[8] In this way, perhaps another comparison can be made to Moses, whom God uses to issue a call to Joshua (Deut. 31:7–8). Deborah, like Moses but not to the same extent, is in communion with God. God imparts his word to Deborah, and she in turn imparts it to others. In essence, God speaks through Deborah to call Barak and to serve as the spiritual leader of the people of Israel.

How Deborah Fulfilled Her Ministry

It's at this juncture that we start to feel like Barak is going to be the one to save us; he will be our judge. But Barak puts a condition on God's call: he will obey if Deborah goes with him. By asking for the presence of the prophet of God, he is in essence asking for the presence of God—or a token of God's presence.[9]

Since Barak puts a condition on his obedience, Deborah prophesies that the Lord will deliver Sisera (Jabin's general) not into Barak's hands but into the hands of an unnamed woman. Original readers and listeners would have taken this as another curveball. So Barak is not our ultimate deliverer? An unnamed woman is going to deliver Israel?

As this leaves us puzzled, the writer wants to emphasize that

Deborah indeed *goes* with Barak. He asks for her to accompany him; she responds, "'Certainly I will go'" (Judg. 4:9). The writer says it once more: "Deborah also went up with him" (v. 10). Indeed, it seems that Barak needs Deborah to go with him to remind him of the Lord's word and promise. She tells him, "'Go! This is the day the LORD has given Sisera into your hands. Has not the LORD gone ahead of you?'" (v. 14). Once more we are reminded of the parallel that Deborah is serving as leader of the people like Jabin, and Barak is serving as general like Sisera. In Judges 5, Deborah uses the metaphor of a mother to describe her leadership of the Jewish people: "Villagers in Israel would not fight; they held back until I, Deborah, arose, until I arose, *a mother in Israel*" (v. 7, emphasis mine).

Barak and his army, with the help of the Lord (who is the real hero of the narrative, of course), overcome and kill every person in Sisera's army except Sisera. In fact, Barak is mentioned for his faith in this battle in Hebrews 11. But as Deborah foretells, Sisera falls into the hands of a woman, who is finally identified: Jael, the wife of Heber the Kenite. This would have been completely unexpected because Jael is not only a woman but a non-Israelite, and her husband has an alliance with Jabin. Yet through this woman, God delivers Israel from the oppression of Sisera and Jabin. In Judges 5, Jael is twice called the most blessed of women.

By the end of Judges 4, we learn who the real judge is: the God of Israel. He is the one who subdues Jabin. Even though Deborah, Barak, and Jael each have a major part to play in the downfall of Israel's enemy, God is the one who speaks through Deborah, is mighty in battle with Barak, and orchestrates Sisera's death at the hands of Jael.

What Can We Learn from Deborah's Calling?

So what can we learn about the calling of women in ministry from this biblical event? First, we should note what the text does and doesn't say about Deborah. The writer emphasizes the fact that she is a woman, but he doesn't make any editorial comments on her gender. The writer also doesn't hide any of the *possibly embarrassing* facts that she is a prophet, that she is judging and leading the people of Israel, and that she is the one imparting the word of the Lord to Barak. It is fair to say that Deborah is viewed *positively*. Many of the judges and leaders of Israel experience some kind of moral failure (just look at David!), but the text gives only a positive portrait of Deborah.

Some argue that this text shows God calls women only when there are no good men to do the job. Their argument is that God uses Deborah to show just how bad things were for God's people in that there were no good men for God to use. But if this is true, why is Barak mentioned for his faith in Hebrews 11? Weren't there other good men besides Barak? What about Deborah's husband? The truth is that we do not know; that is why this is called an argument from silence. I like what New Testament scholar Craig Keener says in response to this argument:

> Even if one were to grant this premise, it would hardly provide an argument against women's ministry today, given the fact that perhaps over half the world's population has yet to hear the gospel of Jesus Christ in a culturally intelligible way and that most of Christ's church and presumably many of its teachers remain too asleep to rise to his call.[10]

Second, Deborah imparts divine speech. This can first be assumed in the fact that she is a prophet—true prophets of the Lord speak from and on behalf of the Lord. We also know this because when she speaks to Barak she says, "'The Lord God has commanded you.'" Her words to Barak are not of her own volition but are a command from the Lord. Not only does she impart divine speech in her own time but also for us today. What she says is Holy Scripture: both in her speech to Barak and in her song. The song is called a song of Deborah and Barak, and we can make two interesting observations. One is that Deborah's name is listed first, which probably means she is the main author of the song. Second, of the few uses of first person in the song, Deborah once refers to herself. Nowhere in the song do we necessarily find Barak speaking in first person. This means that not only did God inspire her words for purposes during her time, but he inspires her words to be part of Holy Scripture for the edification of the church until Jesus returns. Therefore, if anyone argues that women are incapable of speaking or teaching God's Word, they have to reckon with God's use of Deborah *and* with preaching, teaching, and learning from the divinely inspired words of a woman in Judges 4–5.

Third, Deborah is a servant of the Lord. We've already touched on this in the first observation, but I want to say a bit more about it here. As we saw with the men we surveyed in chapters 1 and 2 of this book, Deborah serves on behalf of the Lord, for the people of God, administering the word of God. It's interesting that Deborah calls herself a mother in Israel—this presents the image of one who is caring, providing, nurturing, and watching over her children. The metaphor of a mother is similar to the metaphor of a nurse that Moses uses to describe himself, which is similar to the metaphor of a shepherd.

We don't see in Deborah a modern-day radical feminist who does not want to share her power with men. No; we see her serving the Lord and commissioning Barak because God obviously tells her to do so. We see her prophesying that another woman will be the one to kill Sisera, and she calls that woman, Jael, the most blessed of all tent-dwelling women. In Deborah we see that it is not morally wrong or against God's nature for God to use a woman in a typically male role. She may be an exception, but her story is a testimony to God using the weaker things in this world to despise the wise. Her story is a testimony to what's *most* important to God—to draw people to himself so that he will be their God and they will be his people. And Deborah is another example (just like those who were murderers, enemies of God, last born, poor, and ill-equipped) that God will use whomever he chooses.

THE CALL OF HULDAH

This might be the first time you are hearing of Huldah. Huldah is mentioned in both 2 Kings 22:14–20 (for context, begin in verse 8) and 2 Chronicles 34:22–28. Take a moment to read these passages. Before discussing Huldah, it's worth noting the context in which she is mentioned.

Like the time of the judges, the period of the kings after David is tumultuous. The kingdom is divided after King Solomon's death, and one bad king after another leads the people further away from God. Occasionally a good king rises up in their midst. Prior to 2 Kings 22, a king named Amon reigns in Judah (the southern kingdom) for only two years. He is the son of another evil king, Manasseh. Read the description of Amon: "He did evil in the eyes of the LORD, as his father Manasseh had done. He followed completely the ways of his father, worshiping the idols his father had worshiped, and bowing down to them. He forsook the LORD, the God of his ancestors, and did not walk in obedience to him" (2 Kings 21:20–22). Doesn't this sound like the description of the Israelites in Judges 2:10–14? During this period of evil kings, Josiah, the son of Amon, comes to power.

Josiah, unlike his father and grandfather, is a righteous king. The writer says of him, "He did what was right in the eyes of the LORD" (2 Kings 22:2). During the time of evil kings, the law of Moses (their Scripture) had been forgotten and buried. One of Josiah's reforms is to clean the temple and put back into place right worship of God. However, it isn't until eighteen years into his reign that the book of the law (most likely Deuteronomy[11]) is found as the priests are cleaning the temple. The text says that when Josiah hears the book of the law read to him, he tears his robes—a sign of repentance (2 Kings 22:19). Then he issues the following command to the priest and the secretary: "'Go, inquire of the LORD *for me*, and *for the people*, and *for all Judah*, concerning the words of this book that has been found'" (2 Kings 22:13 ESV, emphasis mine). The priest and the secretary are to find someone who will speak to God on behalf of the people of God, who will interpret the Law, and who will then communicate God's word back to God's people.

It is interesting that although they have the Word of God and hear it read, the king still needs someone to interpret it for him. One scholar explains, "The written Word of itself is not adequate for understanding and practice of the Christian faith. The scroll discovered in the temple was in the language of the people and essentially of their culture. Its significance was not self-evident."[12]

At this juncture in the text, we would expect them to find a male prophet. The well-known prophets at that time are male—Jeremiah and Zephaniah. And just a few chapters (and years!) prior, Josiah's great-grandfather, Hezekiah, inquires of the prophet Isaiah (2 Kings 19:1–7). But instead of going to one of these male prophets, Josiah's envoy consults a woman prophetess by the name of Huldah. Through *this woman* God speaks to King Josiah and thus to the people.

The Ministry of Huldah

Like Deborah, it appears that Huldah is a *true* prophetess of the Lord. In fact, she is the only female prophet mentioned during the period of the kings. In keeping with the tradition of Old Testament prophets, Huldah serves as the "conscience for God's people."[13] She both interprets the Word of God that is read to the king and gives a foretelling word to the king. "Her message is an unequivocal application of the book's message,"[14] and it spurs Josiah to right action and reform. Another scholar says of her, "She is respected as a servant of Yahweh because she is consulted and her interpretation of the law scroll is received as a word from God."[15]

The text then identifies Huldah as the wife of Shallum, who is the keeper of the wardrobe. Some scholars believe that the mention of Shallum's occupation means that he has a relationship with Hilkiah, the high priest, which is perhaps one reason he consults his wife.[16]

What follows is direct speech from Huldah. Three times she uses the refrain, "Thus says the Lord." These words are from a higher authority: God himself. Huldah speaks on God's behalf. Also, from her speech it seems apparent God has foretold her about their visit and the repentance of Josiah. God has prepared her for this moment. This is no accident; God has arranged these events as he sees fit. Old Testament scholar Paul House says, "Once again God's word has been faithfully and accurately proclaimed, this time as an interpretation of the *written Word*."[17] Like Deborah's words, Huldah's words become Holy Scripture.

However, if you read the rest of Josiah's story, you'll notice a tension between what Huldah foretells about Josiah's death and his actual death. Huldah prophesies that he will be "buried in peace" (2 Kings 22:20). But Josiah dies in battle at the hands of the Egyptian king (2 Kings 23:28–30). For some, this is a problem. But the text does not present this as a problem or claim that Huldah's prophecy is inaccurate. Josiah dies during a time of peace for Israel, and he is given a proper burial in Jerusalem. As Huldah foretells, his eyes do not see all the disaster God brings on "this place" (2 Kings 22:20).

What Can We Learn from Huldah's Calling?

What can we learn about a biblical case for or against women in ministry from Huldah? First, Huldah is another *positive* example of God using a woman in a typical male role in a male-dominated society. Again, there's no editorial comment to explain why God would use a woman, or to say she is a rare exception not to be modeled. No issue is made of her gender. Rather, she is viewed positively as a true prophet of the Lord who accurately interprets and prophesies as God has spoken to her.

Second, her call is to prophesy and interpret to instruct and lead to right action a male king, all the people of Judah, and us today. Her words are part of the divinely inspired Word of God that we call Scripture. The words she speaks go beyond Josiah and the people of her day to you and me today. This is important because God is *still* using a woman, Huldah, to teach us about himself and his Word. If God uses the mouth of a woman to *inspire* Scripture, then—using a greater-to-lesser argument—it is very plausible that he uses women today to *interpret* and *teach* his inspired Word.

OTHER OLD TESTAMENT WOMEN CALLED BY GOD

God has always included women in his plan. For one, we are created in his image just as men are created. We read about how God uses women like Rahab, Tamar, Esther, and Ruth to bring about his plan of salvation (three of these women are included in the genealogy of Jesus in Matthew 1!). Esther serves as queen, and Miriam and Isaiah's wife are prophetesses. Then there are other women like Hannah, through whom the Lord speaks divinely inspired Scripture (1 Sam. 2:1–10). We also could spend time looking at Abigail, whom the Lord sends and through whom he speaks to David to spare him from bloodguilt. David recognizes the authority from which Abigail speaks and blesses the Lord and her because of it. He also blesses Abigail for her discernment and does as she says (1 Sam. 25:2–35).

It is worth noting, however, that we do not find examples of women serving as priests. This office is reserved only for men, even though in other cultic Ancient Near Eastern religions women did serve as priestesses. However, Moses, Joshua, David, Samuel, and many other prophets also did not serve as priests. The story of Scripture focuses more on the stories of prophets and shepherds (kings) than the stories of priests. Also, Jeremiah is a priest when he is called to be a prophet, and the book of Jeremiah is focused on his time as a prophet, not as a priest. The role of priests in the Old Testament context is not equivocal to the role of ministers in churches today (nor even in the New Testament!). For example, the most important role of the priest was the offering of sacrifices. With Jesus Christ having replaced the temple, this primary role of the priest is void. So while it is worth noting, it is not a significant point *against* women in ministry.

As we look forward from the Old Testament to the New, we must ask if the use of women in these ways continues or ends in the New Testament. Let's turn to the prophet Joel, whose prophecy from the Lord gives us a grid through which we can and perhaps should read the New Testament to answer these questions.

> And afterward, I will pour out my Spirit on all people. Your sons
> and daughters will prophesy, your old men will dream dreams,

your young men will see visions. Even on my servants, both men
and women, I will pour out my Spirit in those days. (Joel 2:28–29)

Just prior to these verses, Joel has seen a vision of God restoring his covenant with Israel, which will bring both spiritual and physical blessings—peace, food, rain, no shame. When the people have truly turned back to God, his first promise is that he will pour out his Spirit. The term *pour out* indicates that he is not going to give just a taste of his Spirit; rather, he is going to pour out the fullness of his Spirit, the third person of the Trinity. Giving his Spirit is giving his presence—giving himself.

Who will receive God's Spirit? *All* his people. So that we don't assume that this gift is not truly all-inclusive, God further clarifies: sons and daughters (men *and* women), old and young, master and slave. God's Spirit will not be reserved for only *some* priests, prophets, and kings—those called by God to serve him for the people of God. Rather, as Old Testament scholar Douglas Stuart says, "*All* of God's people will have *all* they need of God's Spirit" (emphasis mine).[18]

"Sons and daughters" is another way of saying men and women, for everyone is a son or a daughter. Both men and women will receive equal portions of the same Spirit. Men won't receive more and women less. Men won't receive a different Spirit than women will. Because they will receive equal measures of the same Spirit, all of God's children—both genders—will prophesy, dream dreams, and see visions.

Now, as we end with the prophecy from Joel, we are given a vision for the new era of the Spirit of God being poured out on all God's people, resulting in all God's people having some manifestation or proof of this (i.e., prophecy, visions). Remember what happens when the Spirit of God comes down at Pentecost (Acts 2:1–13)? All the people who receive the Spirit speak in tongues. Peter rightfully understands that event in light of Joel 2:28–29. We will explore this more in the next chapter.

Some scholars, like Stuart, interpret this prophecy as having implications for how we view ministry today. He says:

> For Christians the significance of this expectation should be clear. Those who live in the age of the Spirit cannot expect God to restrict any ministry of the Spirit from anyone simply because he or she is old or young, male or female, or of high or low standing socially. Where churches attempt to do this, they risk missing the fullness of God's blessing.[19]

WHAT HAVE WE LEARNED?

Remember the question we are asking: Does God call women to gospel ministry? In the Old Testament we see cases where women are involved in a form of ministry dominated by males. We see that God uses women to speak the inspired words of God; we have Scripture spoken by women. We see that God involves women in the working out of his ongoing work of salvation throughout history. (This process is often known as salvation history.)

The questions for us as we go into the next chapter are as follows: Does God continue to use women in the New Testament like he does in the Old Testament? Do the New Testament examples of women increase and develop in areas of ministry or lessen? If gospel ministry is done in partnership with and under the supervision of the Spirit, then what does that mean for women in light of Joel 2:28–29?

Let's turn now to the New Testament as we continue seeking to answer the question, does God call and use women in vocational, gospel ministry?

> Now to him who is able to do far more abundantly than all that we ask or think, according to the power at work within us, to him be glory in the church and in Christ Jesus throughout all generations, forever and ever. Amen. (Eph. 3:20–21 ESV).

REFLECTION QUESTIONS

1. I began by saying that church and ministry today are much different from what we find in Scripture. How so? Do you think there is a larger vocational space for women to serve in ministry today? Explain. If so, how does that encourage you as you pursue God's call?

2. What do you think of the argument that God calls women only when there are no good men to do the job? Was Craig Keener's explanation to the contrary convincing? Why or why not?

3. What did you learn from the Old Testament women we examined that helps you in your calling and ministry?

DISCUSSION QUESTIONS

1. Who is your favorite Old Testament woman and why?

2. What do you think Deborah, Huldah, Abigail, and other Old Testament women have to teach us today?

3. What questions and/or insights do you have from Joel 2:28–29?

PERSONAL EXERCISES

1. How have you understood the role of women in Scripture and in ministry up to this point in your life?

Put in writing your beliefs or assumptions and any questions you have.

2. Take a look at one or two other Old Testament women called by God for his purposes. Choose one (or more!) and make notes about their calling and purpose in salvation history. Reflect on them in light of the women we discussed in this chapter.

MINISTRY SPOTLIGHT:

DEBORAH LEIGHTON

The daughter of an ordained minister, Deborah Leighton was twenty-one years old when she first heard a call to ministry. As a student at Wheaton College in Illinois, Deborah argued her way into an upper-level class on the Gospel of John with Dr. Gary Burge. For the final project of the class, Deborah was assigned to write a paper on John 11. The Sunday before the paper was due, she took a break from writing to go to church to worship.

"While I waited to receive communion, I was praying and felt overwhelmed by the Holy Spirit. I sensed the Lord pointing out how much I loved studying Scripture," Deborah said. "It was as though he said, 'I made you to love this. This is meant to be for my people.' I did love studying and could easily live within academia, but I felt like the Lord was saying that any insight into Scripture would best be shared through church ministry."

Though this probably was a clear call to ministry, Deborah had her doubts. After graduating from college, she moved to New York City to pursue an acting career. But two-and-a-half years into her time there, the Lord changed her desires. Acting was no longer her dream; instead, she wanted to serve people and sensed it was time to go to seminary.

Deborah went to Trinity School for Ministry in Ambridge, Pennsylvania, an evangelical seminary in the Anglican tradition. She loved learning biblical Greek and doing exegesis, and the "fishbowl" of the seminary community prepared Deborah for the "fishbowl" of ministry.

While in seminary, Deborah began the ordination process. Each diocese within the Episcopal Church or within the Anglican Church of North America (ACNA) has a slightly different process for ordination. The process Deborah went through involved a parish discernment committee, approval by the vestry, approval by the bishop and diocesan discernment committee, a physical exam, a psychological exam, a background check, a few personality tests, and about twenty written and oral exams. It all took five years.

"While this process can be long and frustrating for many people, I didn't mind it at the time because I truly wanted to discern correctly if I was called to ordained ministry," she said. "This process is so involved because Anglican ministers are ordained for life, unlike most other Protestant ministers, who are ordained for specific ministries."

After ordination in 2009, Deborah served as an ACNA church planter in western Massachusetts for three years. Then, in 2012, she came on staff at the Cathedral Church of the Advent in Birmingham, Alabama. She transitioned from being the only minister on staff at a tiny parish to being one of five ordained ministers on staff at a large parish.

As Canon Missioner and Director of Women's Ministries at the Advent, Deborah leads multiple Bible studies, teaches Sunday school, oversees mission and outreach and women's ministries, meets pastorally with parishioners, and preaches on occasion throughout the year, among many other pastoral duties.

When I asked her what she would say to you, Deborah responded, "Lifelong vocational ministry is in itself a daring calling—one that will require far more from you than you can ever produce naturally. Thank goodness for this, because it will force you to put your whole trust in Christ! He is the one who does the work through you, and he will do work in you as a result. At the beginning of your call, and every step along the way, consider meditating on Romans 8:33–34 (ESV): 'Who shall bring any charge against God's elect? It is God who justifies. Who is to condemn? Christ Jesus is the one who died—more than that, who was raised—who is at the right hand of God, who indeed is interceding for us.' Stepping out to do ministry is an act of wild faith, especially for women. Perhaps you are in fact called to live such a daring life to the glory of God?"

CHAPTER 4

The Calling of Women in the New Testament

When we transition from the Old Testament to the New, we immediately notice that something has changed. God has entered the story in a unique way! He is *Emmanuel*—God with us. In the previous chapter, we concluded by asking if God's use of women in ministry has continued, if it has stalled, or if it has changed. We ended by considering Joel 2:28–29: "And afterward, I will pour out my Spirit on all people. Your sons and daughters will prophesy, your old men will dream dreams, your young men will see visions. Even on my servants, both men and women, I will pour out my Spirit in those days."

As we continue to explore the role of women in the outworking of God's purposes in salvation, we will dig deeper, looking at Mary, the mother of Jesus, and several other women in the Gospels, including Priscilla and the women of Romans 16. We'll ask this question: *Does God still call and use women in gospel ministry today?* In the following chapter, we will discuss the most frequently cited passage on this topic, one that seems to restrict the ministry of women in the teaching and communication of God's Word.

Our framework for understanding the work of ministry in Luke and Acts is found in Acts 2 in the fulfillment of the prophecy of Joel.[1] It is within this context—that the age of the Spirit has come, and sons and daughters will prophesy—that I propose we will understand the ministry of Mary and the other women in Luke and the Acts of the Apostles.

THE CALL OF MARY, THE MOTHER OF JESUS

Partly as a reaction to some Roman Catholic practices, Protestants tend to ignore Mary. In fact, you may be wondering why she is included in a chapter on ministry calling when her main call appears to have been to give birth. Nevertheless, her importance is not lost on New Testament scholars like Joel Green, who says the following: "God has given his favor to one who had no claim to worthy status, raised her up from a position of lowliness, and has chosen her to have a central role in salvation history."[2] The centrality of her role lies not only in her giving birth to the Son of God but also in her Spirit-filled interpretation of the birth of Jesus. Let's look at Luke 1:26–66. As with Deborah and Huldah, I will walk through the passage carefully, then draw some conclusions at the end.

The book of Luke opens with two parallel birth announcement scenes: the angel Gabriel first appears to Zechariah, announcing the birth of John the Baptist (Luke 1:5–23) and then to Mary, announcing the birth of Jesus (vv. 26–38). Mary is juxtaposed with Zechariah here. Zechariah is a priest; Mary is a virgin living in Nazareth. Zechariah's encounter with God's messenger occurs in the temple, which sits at the heart of Jerusalem, the holy city. Mary's encounter with God's messenger occurs far away from Jerusalem in a town considered by many to be despicable, of little significance, and unclean.[3] As we will see, Zechariah, though a priest and a righteous man, responds to Gabriel's message with unbelief, whereas Mary, an insignificant country girl, responds in belief.

Our passage begins with Gabriel being sent to Mary. We are told in Luke 1:19 that Gabriel stands in the presence of God. He is God's special messenger, or herald, of good news. Gabriel's status probably means he is an archangel or a high-ranking angel.[4] Luke wants us to pay attention to the significance of the event, for this news is of such importance that God has sent one of the angels who stands in his presence to deliver this message on his behalf.

Before we are given Mary's name, we are told something about her: she is a virgin. In fact, her virginity is mentioned three times, in verses 27 (twice) and 34. What is the author trying to convey by reiterating her virginity? This is important so that there will be no doubt of the forthcoming miracle that her son is conceived by the Holy Spirit and is thus the Son of God. Mary's virginity also means she is young, probably twelve or thirteen years old.[5] But it's also almost certain that Luke is making the connection between Mary's virginity and the prophecy of Isaiah 7:14: "Therefore the Lord himself will give you a sign: The virgin will conceive and give birth to a son, and will call him Immanuel." The appearance of Gabriel and the emphasis on Mary's virginity also serve as signs to us that God is about to intervene in human history.

The Ministry of Mary

So far, all we know of Mary is that she is a virgin country girl of little significance who is engaged to a man named Joseph. Yet when Gabriel greets her, he immediately announces the reversal of her status. Who is Mary from God's perspective? We learn that God has chosen Mary, given his favor to her, and is with her (Luke 1:28). When Gabriel tells Mary that the Lord is with her, what does that remind you of? The presence of God always accompanies the calling of God! When God calls someone to serve on his behalf in the working out of salvation history, he always gives his presence.

Despite her belief, Mary is afraid. How often have you felt afraid in response to your calling? In response, Gabriel reiterates once more that she has found favor with God. How can she know she has found God's favor? Because, as Gabriel says, she will bear God's Son. Gabriel's message begins with her role in this miraculous event: you will conceive, you will bear a son, and you will name him Jesus (Luke 1:31). Then Gabriel transitions to God's role in this event: he will give Jesus the throne of David; God the Son will reign over the house of Jacob forever; the Holy Spirit will come upon Mary (vv. 32–35). In this, one of the greatest acts in human and salvation history, God chooses to become incarnate, specifically through one woman: Mary.

Mary, like Moses and Jeremiah, responds to the call with a

question: "How will this be . . . since I am a virgin?" (Luke 1:34). Unlike Zechariah, who asks a question out of unbelief (v. 18), Mary's question is not because of doubt; rather, it appears she doesn't understand. We know this because after Zechariah's question, Gabriel reprimands him for not believing and causes him to fall mute. Conversely, when Mary asks her question, Gabriel neither reproves her for unbelief nor punishes her. In fact, later, Elizabeth, through the inspiration of the Holy Spirit, commends Mary for her belief in Gabriel's message from the Lord (v. 45).

Mary's question also allows Gabriel to give her—and us—more information about the miracle that is going to take place. The Holy Spirit will be poured out on Mary (v. 35). Mary—low in rank because of her age, family, and gender—will experience the outpouring of the Holy Spirit long before the Holy Spirit is given to God's people at Pentecost. The power of the Most High will overshadow her. These two statements are parallel each other and describe the same divine act, but this second phrase especially reminds us of another time in the past when the glory of the Lord came down—in Exodus. When the glory of the Lord came down in the appearance of a cloud over the Tent of Meeting, it was such that not even Moses could enter into the tabernacle! Mary will be overshadowed by the presence of the Most High, and the Holy Spirit will be poured out on her—yet she will not be consumed! And—don't miss this—she is the first one to experience "Pentecost" and the beginning of the fulfillment of Joel 2:28–29!

The coming of the presence of the Most High will result in the miraculous conception of the Son of God. He will be called holy because he is God, for only God is holy. The sign for Mary that this will come to pass is that her relative Elizabeth is pregnant at an old age. This is a sign probably because it recalls to mind another time when God intervenes in human history to bring about his plan through Sarah, who becomes pregnant past childbearing age. Gabriel ends with the words, "For nothing will be impossible with God" (Luke 1:37 ESV). What seems like an impossibility for Mary is not impossible for God. When God chooses to act, nothing can stand in his way.

How Mary Fulfilled Her Ministry

Mary responds to the Lord's call in obedience and submission. At face value, the fact that Mary calls herself God's servant may not seem like much, but this has several implications. First, by offering herself to God in his service, she is laying down her rights and even jeopardizing the future she thought she would have with Joseph. When she says yes to God, she doesn't know how the rest of the story will go—if Joseph, or any man, will still have her. Second, a slave's status in ancient Rome corresponds to the status of his/her master.[6] So to be in the service of *God* means that her status actually improves! Third, as we have seen thus far, the title "servant of the Lord" is used by all of those who are called by God—Moses, Joshua, David, and Paul are just a few examples. Green says that when the Greek word for slave is used in connection with God or the Lord, it is referring to "a person who has been commissioned and endowed for a special role in the divine plan."[7] He goes on to say,

> In his characterization of Mary as "slave of the Lord," Luke has begun to undercut the competitive maneuvering for positions of status prevalent in the first-century Mediterranean world. Mary, who seemed to measure low in any ranking—age, family, heritage, gender, and so on—turns out to be the one favored by God, the one who finds her status and identity in her obedience to God and participation of his salvific will.[8]

Sometime after the angel leaves Mary, she goes to visit her cousin Elizabeth. Before we go on, though, take a few minutes to read Luke 1:39–45, if you haven't already. I'd like to make a couple of quick comments about this passage. First, Elizabeth is, like Mary, filled with the Holy Spirit prior to Pentecost. Her speech to Mary is inspired by the Lord, meaning she is speaking as God's mouthpiece. What we have in Elizabeth is yet another example of a woman being used by God to discern and speak the word of God.

Second, in ancient times, the societal rule was that the lesser person must greet the greater person, as Mary does when she enters Elizabeth's home.[9] But Elizabeth turns the table and greets Mary! In fact, not only does she greet Mary, but she also blesses her—or rather, calls her blessed—which is another sign of the reversal of Mary's status.

THE MAGNIFICAT: MARY'S SONG

Mary's Song, also commonly known as the *Magnificat*, is theologically and compositionally beautiful. Following Elizabeth's inspired words, Mary is herself inspired and speaks a word of the Lord (Luke 1:46–55). Luke isn't just interested in telling us the bare facts of the events surrounding Jesus' birth; he wants his readers to understand the theological meaning of Jesus' birth. Mary's inspired words serve as an interpretation of the preceding events. By including her song in his Gospel, Luke, under the direction of the Holy Spirit, demonstrates how important it is for us to understand the significance of this event.

Mary begins her song by recognizing her reversal of status. God has taken someone who is lowly and has exalted her. Not only has Elizabeth called her blessed, but generations to follow will too! Mary recognizes that the significance of this act of God is not only for those of her generation but for people to come. *This has nothing to do with Mary earning God's favor, but is solely because of God's mercy and grace to Mary.* Thus, she praises him. Her song is reminiscent of the psalms of David. It stands alongside the other great songs in Scripture, those of Moses, Miriam, Deborah, and Asaph, as well as the prayer of Hannah. For this reason, Green calls her song a "virtual collage of biblical texts."[10]

Mary rightly recognizes that God's act of mercy toward her is an act of mercy toward Israel. What begins as praise for what God has done for Mary is expanded to Israel. Put another way, Mary is a representative of what God is also doing for Israel and thereby us.

This song is rightfully a song about who God is and why we should praise him. He is both the One who executes justice toward the prideful and powerful and the One who shows mercy to the lowly and hungry. The God Mary praises—our God—is the One who reverses worldly statuses. Green says, "The God Mary praises is the covenant-making God, the God who acts out of his own self-giving nature to embrace men and women in relationship. God remembers . . . and acts."[11]

What Can We Learn from Mary's Calling?

We give a lot of space to Mary because (a) she's given thirty verses in the first chapter of Luke; (b) she is called by God for a specific role that is pivotal to the salvation narrative; and (c) her words are Spirit-inspired. Let's summarize now the lessons we can learn from Mary's story.

First, Luke spends a good amount of time on Mary's role in the birth of Jesus in his narrative, including direct speech from Mary. We would probably not expect to read so much about Mary or even hear from her directly in a patriarchal culture, but that isn't the case here. Luke, through the Holy Spirit, recognizes her importance in the advent of God's Son, her faith, and her inspired words. The ultimate goal of this is to demonstrate God's reversal of the world's paradigms, including the reversal of women.

Second, like the many others we have covered thus far in the book, God singularly calls Mary—even sending one of his highest-ranking angels—to serve him on his behalf for the people of God.

Third, Mary has a unique relationship with God. She receives the Holy Spirit before anyone else at Pentecost. Besides Moses, she is the only other person in Scripture who experiences the glory of the Lord in such an intimate way and is not consumed. Jesus' flesh, DNA, features, and human mannerisms all come from his mother, Mary. God the Son takes on *her* human flesh. God enjoins himself to a woman to share in her flesh. And because of the Holy Spirit and God's anointing on her, she speaks the inspired words of God. She speaks faithfully and truthfully and even explains and applies Old Testament Scripture in her song! Every time we study Mary's words to Gabriel and her song, we sit at the feet of a female teacher, one who is inspired by God.

Fourth, as already mentioned, the title "servant" is used by and of those called by God into service for the people of God. Using the title servant puts Mary into that special group of people called by God.

Fifth, Mary's obedience is a step of faith and a sacrifice. In Luke 1:34, Mary says, "'How will this be?'" By verse 38, Mary says, "'Let it be'" (ESV). Not long ago, I was telling my former preaching professor, Robert Smith Jr., about how God was leading me in my calling. I told him I did not know how it was going to come to fruition other than by God doing it. He quoted these two verses to me and said, "Mary went from 'How will this be?' to 'Let it be.' You don't know how, but you know Who. And you say to the Who, 'Let it be.'" By Mary saying, "'Let it be to me according to your word,'" she risks losing her fiancé, her place in her town and family, her reputation, and perhaps even her life! She has no idea how everything will turn out, but she obeys in faith because she trusts God. While we will not be called by God in this particular way or to this extent, Mary's obedience and faith encourage us to respond in the same manner to our own callings, even when we do not know the how and even if it first appears the call might jeopardize the future we have planned for ourselves.

Sixth, an important theme throughout the Gospel of Luke and especially in Mary's song, is that of God reversing worldly statuses. Mary was a nobody—a young Galilean peasant girl who was about to be married. Why would God's favor fall upon her? Why would God choose her? How could she be qualified to speak divinely inspired words that we now call Scripture? Because God doesn't look at the things that the world looks at. Because, as Paul tells us in 1 Corinthians, "God chose the foolish things of the world to shame the wise; God chose the weak things of the world to shame the strong" (1 Cor. 1:27).

What does Mary's story have to do with our calls to ministry? I recently sat in a seminary classroom as young women shared their calling experiences with their male-student colleagues. One young woman said she remembered encountering women who, because of their church context, thought that to pursue formal ministry was to sin against God. Mary's story, like Deborah's, Huldah's, and others', is another wonderful example that God uses women—even enjoins himself to them—to bring about the ministry of Jesus Christ. Mary's story should give us great encouragement, because the God in Mary's story is the same God who is involved in our stories!

OTHER WOMEN IN THE GOSPELS

We don't find another calling story quite like Mary's in the rest of the Gospels. But what we do find are women disciples and a positive portrayal of women. Early in the Gospel of John, we read a long narrative about Jesus and the Samaritan woman (John 4:1–42). The Samaritan woman is the earliest example of an evangelist we are given in Jesus' ministry. Before we are told that the disciples go out proclaiming the good news, this woman—after being changed by the good news—goes back to her town, tells people the gospel, and brings them with her to meet Jesus. The simple fact that Jesus chooses to encounter this woman means he also knows and intends for her to be able to bring many in her town to belief in him.

In Luke 8:1–3 we are given a broader picture of the people accompanying Jesus in his ministry. Luke tells us that in addition to the twelve disciples, a number of women are "with him." Green suggests that the phrase "with Jesus" is another way to say that they are his disciples.[12] To include women among his traveling entourage, along with men, is remarkable given the culture. Keener says, "Women as disciples of teachers were rare or unheard of in most philosophic and rhetorical schools of antiquity."[13] The women providing for the group out of their means (v. 3) is an act of worship and gratitude for what God has done for them. Simply by mentioning this, Luke is letting us know how important these women are to the ministry of Jesus.

In examining just one of the Gospels, we see that God uses women in salvation history, most notably Mary in the birth of Jesus, and that Jesus involves women in his ministry and includes them as disciples. A Samaritan woman is the first recorded evangelist; Mary, the sister of Martha, sits at the feet of Jesus in the posture of a disciple; and women are the first eyewitnesses to Jesus' resurrection, just to give a few examples.

Now we come to the beginning of the early church, the period after Jesus' ascension. Here we can ask, what is the role of women in early Christianity? Does the trajectory continue such that women are increasingly involved in the work of the church? Or is the opposite true? Remember that the Bible is not written to make a case for or against women in ministry! The authors' intent—filled with the inspiration of the Holy Spirit—is to tell us the story of redemption. However, we are given glimpses of what women are doing in the ministry of the early church. The remaining sections of this chapter are going to survey women who are involved in the ministry of the early church. I hope they encourage you as positive examples from Scripture.

THE CALL OF PRISCILLA

We first meet Priscilla in Acts 18 along with her husband, Aquila. They are exiled from their home in Rome because of a decree expelling the Jews. Luke, the writer of Acts, tells us that Paul meets them at Corinth (Acts 18:1–2). We cannot be certain, but he probably has heard they are Christians, and the text says Paul shares the profession of tent-making with them. By verse 18, we are certain that Priscilla and Aquila are Christians and Paul's co-workers, for he takes them with him when he sails for Syria and leaves them in Ephesus to do ministry. We know from Paul's other letters (1 Corinthians, Romans, and 2 Timothy) that they are actively doing ministry together, including hosting a church in their home.

The Ministry of Priscilla

Scripture does not give us a neat and tidy calling story regarding Priscilla. However, I want to focus on three aspects concerning Priscilla so that we do not write her off as an inactive participant in ministry. First, five of the seven times she is mentioned in Scripture, Priscilla is listed *before* her husband.[14] Keener says, "Name sequence can be important, especially when it diverges from the anticipated ancient norm of naming the husband first."[15] So what do we make of Priscilla's name being listed before her husband's? Many scholars say this gives us a strong clue that Priscilla (also sometimes called Prisca) has the more important role in Paul's and the early church's ministry. In the three instances when their ministry is mentioned, Priscilla is always mentioned first.

In Acts 18:24–28, which we will look at momentarily, Priscilla is named before Aquila when Luke tells us that they take Apollos aside and instruct him. Some scholars, including Keener, say this means she is the primary teacher of Apollos.[16] While we cannot make an argument for women in ministry based on this point alone, it is worth noting because it is unusual to find a wife's name listed before her husband's in both Hebrew and Greek culture.

Second, Priscilla *instructs* Apollos. What is interesting is that Apollos isn't some simpleton. He "was a *learned* man," "with a *thorough knowledge* of the Scriptures," "*instructed* in the way of the Lord," who "spoke with *great fervor* and taught about Jesus *accurately*," and "began to speak *boldly* in the synagogue" (Acts 18:24–26, emphasis mine). Luke stresses that Apollos is well-educated! However, as verse 25 says, Apollos only knew of the baptism of John. Therefore, what Priscilla and Aquila are doing is instructing him on the basics of the gospel. Eventually Apollos is sent by the church in Ephesus to do missionary work, and Apollos has a fruitful ministry in Corinth. It is interesting to contrast this passage with 1 Tim. 2:11–15 (chapter 5), because the latter appears to deny women instructing men. Yet, here in Acts, with the name of Priscilla at the beginning, it appears this is exactly what is happening. We have to take this into account when we read 1 Timothy 2.

Third, Priscilla is called Paul's "co-worker" in Romans 16:3. This attribution is used only to describe those who are participants in Paul's ministry of spreading the gospel. It's a designation mostly used for men but also used for a few women like Euodia and

Syntyche (Phil. 4:2–3) in addition to Priscilla. While we aren't given many details about Priscilla's ministry, we do know she and Aquila work as a missionary husband-wife team, and her ministry isn't passive or behind the scenes.

In conclusion, Priscilla disciples, instructs and teaches, evangelizes, and co-leads a church in her house. Both her husband and Paul commend and encourage her in ministry of the gospel.

THE CALLINGS OF WOMEN IN ROMANS 16

Let's briefly consider several of the other women Paul mentions in Romans 16. Paul writes a letter to the churches in Rome, and he concludes by offering greetings to Christians he knows. What's remarkable about this list is that Paul mentions nine women, five of whom are commended for their ministry.

Phoebe

Paul begins his greetings with a woman, Phoebe, to whom he in fact gives the longest greeting. Paul starts by commending Phoebe to the Roman Christians, exhorting them to welcome her. Immediately he tells them who she is: a deacon (or deaconess). The word *deacon* can also be translated as "servant" or "minister." When it is used to refer to an office (like we find in 1 Timothy), instead of saying "servant," we translate it "deacon." There is some debate as to whether the word as it is used here means Phoebe holds an office in the church, given that he uses the term in relation to the church, saying she is a "deacon of the church in Cenchreae," or simply is a servant as any other Christian.[17] However, even more conservative New Testament scholars believe that it's most likely Phoebe held the office of deacon in the church.[18]

According to Romans 16:2, Phoebe is also a "benefactor" or "patron" (*prostatis*), which means she supports Paul's ministry financially. In antiquity, "the title is one of authority and honor."[19] Some scholars believe it is most likely Paul urges the Roman Christians to welcome and take care of her because she is going to deliver his letter to them.[20] Delivering a letter in the ancient world is not like serving as a postal worker who hands over a letter and then leaves. The letter deliverer often serves as an interpreter on behalf of the sender.[21] This means Paul likely talked through his letter with Phoebe. If there is some debate in the Roman church or questions concerning what Paul means in his letter, Phoebe is the one who will answer them. By delivering the letter, then, Phoebe is not only identified as trustworthy but as someone to whom Paul gives authority to interpret his letter for the Roman Christians.[22] Phoebe is probably the first interpreter of Romans! While we are not given all the details of Phoebe's ministry, we know she plays an important role in her local church and in Paul's ministry.

Junia

In verse 7, Paul commends another possible husband and wife team—Adronicus and Junia—as being "outstanding among the apostles." Another translation of the word is "prominent." This verse has caused many problems for interpreters who have a certain view on what women cannot do in areas of ministry. Why? Because if we read Scripture as the NIV translates it, then a woman can be an apostle. For those of us living in the twenty-first century, the apostolic significance might be lost on us. What is an apostle?

An apostle is someone who has seen the resurrected Jesus and has received from him the commission to take the gospel to others.[23] Of course, we normally think of apostles as the twelve disciples and Paul, but others are also called apostles, although they do not have the same authority as the Twelve.[24] Apostles have authority in areas of preaching, teaching, and evangelizing that is recognized by the church because Jesus himself gives them authority.

For a woman to have this type of authority in the church has been problematic throughout church history, so much so that some people have attempted to claim that Junia is a male. However, sufficient evidence has been given to disprove this. Another way in which some scholars have softened the meaning of the text has been to interpret the preposition "among" in the verse as "by" instead, which

which would change the meaning from Junia being esteemed *among* the apostles to being esteemed *by* the apostles. Those who argue for this hold the minority view. For a fuller explanation of why, see the sidebar on "Junia and Biblical Scholarship." If we take Junia as an apostle, even as half of a husband-wife apostle team, then we have another example of a woman involved in ministry—a ministry made up of mostly men—and one with authority.

JUNIA AND BIBLICAL SCHOLARSHIP

From the thirteenth century to the twentieth century, scholars and scribes regularly claimed Junia was a man because they could not accept the idea that a woman had been given the title of apostle. By simply changing an accent mark, they solved the problem, turning *Junia* (a woman's name) into *Junias* (a man's name). You can still see this modification if you read the Revised Standard Version's translation of the Bible. Not only is Junias used instead of Junia, but the word *men* is added to the verse to stress the view that these were two men, not a man and a woman.

Prior to the thirteenth century, many of those writing during the early church period, including the church fathers, understood Junia to be a woman. The accent mark that turned Junia into Junias was not present during this time. New Testament scholar Frank Thielman writes in his upcoming commentary on Romans, "There are no examples of the masculine name 'Junias' from Greco-Roman antiquity, however, making it certain that patristic commentators prior to the middle ages and recent interpreters are correct in identifying 'Junia' as a woman." In other words, the name Junias didn't exist in that period, making it undeniable that Junia was indeed a woman.

Even with the evidence that Junia was a woman, some scholars have tried to soften the text by suggesting that Junia was not an apostle. How? It comes down to the translation of a single preposition in the original Greek. The NIV translates this as "among," meaning Junia was prominent among the apostles, which indicates that *she* is an apostle, one of the group. Those who disagree with this position have argued that the Greek preposition does not mean "among" but "by." This translation of the preposition subtly changes the meaning of the verse to mean that Junia was esteemed *by* the apostles—that Junia was prominent in the eyes of the apostles. You see this reflected in the following Bible translations: the Holman Christian Standard Bible, the English Standard Version, and the New English Translation.

While this second translation is popular among those who do not want to acknowledge Junia as an apostle, many scholars today—even several conservative voices—agree that the latter view is the least likely of the two translations. The more natural reading is simply "among." Since the early church fathers spoke Greek as their first language, we should look at how *they* understood the preposition. When we look at their commentaries on Romans, we see that they consistently translated this word as "among" and understood Junia to be an apostle (Origen, Theodoret of Cyrus, and John Chrysostom). For more details in support of this view, see Frank Thielman's commentary on *Romans* in the Exegetical Commentary on the New Testament (Grand Rapids: Zondervan, 2018), chapter 16.

Other Women in Romans and Philippians

In addition to Phoebe and Junia, Paul greets four more women—Mary, Tryphena, Tryphosa, and Persis—and commends their "hard work" in the Lord. In fact, the only people Paul commends for their hard work in the Lord are these four women. Remember (chapter 2) that Paul calls himself a "worker of the Lord" and often uses the language of work or service to describe his own calling as an apostle. While we do not know what shape their ministry takes, Paul's commendation gives us a snapshot of just how involved in ministry women are in the period of the New Testament. The point here is not the details of their work but the fact that they are *involved*.

Paul commends the ministry of two other women in Philippians 4:2–3. However, his reason for mentioning Euodia and Syntyche is a negative one—they are having a disagreement. And this must be no small disagreement! It is big enough that word has reached Paul, and he feels he must address it in his letter to the church. Paul wants these women to reconcile because they "have contended at my side in the cause of the gospel." The word translated "contended" is a gladiatorial word also translated as "fighting alongside." The ESV renders this verse as these women laboring "side by side" with Paul in the gospel. These women are not passive partakers in Paul's ministry nor have they sat on the fringes. They have fought side by side with Paul in ministry in Philippi. So even though they are being exhorted by Paul, they nevertheless are shown to be workers for and ministers of the gospel.

WHAT CAN WE LEARN FROM THIS?

What ministry looks like for women and which roles are open to women is a topic of debate in our culture and must be worked out within your church tradition and according to your conscience, which is captive to Scripture. But what we have seen in this chapter and the previous one is this: God calls women and employs them in his service. His plan has always included women, not merely as recipients of grace or mere spectators but as active participants. He's been doing it since the beginning with Eve. She was the suitable helper God knew Adam needed.

One way Scripture describes the church is by using the metaphor of the family of God. Adam and Eve are the first family; they are also the first church. As we enter the New Testament, we see the family of God metaphor really taking shape (Gal. 6:10; 1 Thess. 4:10; Heb. 2:11; 1 Pet. 2:17; 5:9). Just as a church family needs spiritual fathers to lead, guide, and teach, likewise it needs spiritual mothers to lead, guide, and teach. If we believe that the best situation for children is to have a father and a mother at home, the children and family of God also need fathers and mothers to lead them spiritually in the way of truth.

Throughout Scripture we have examples of God raising up women to serve as helpers and colleagues in the service of God to take the word of God to the people of God. What is even more exciting is that we see an increase in the number of women involved in a ministry of the word for the people of God from the Old Testament to the New Testament.

Let's consider the women we have surveyed in the latter half of this chapter. Women in Paul's ministry serve as teachers/instructors, evangelists, disciple makers, co-leaders of churches, deacons, benefactors, interpreters of Paul's letters, apostles, and Paul's co-workers in ministry. He employs the words *servant* and *co-laborer* to describe many of these women. They are serving side by side with men: Priscilla with Aquila, Junia with Andronicus, Phoebe with Paul, for example. What Paul does in employing women as co-laborers in gospel ministry mimics what Jesus himself does. Women serve on Jesus' ministerial team. They sit at his feet as his disciples; they minister *to* him and *with* his other disciples. God entrusts them to be heralds and interpreters of good news concerning Jesus, from Mary who interprets the incarnation, to the Samaritan woman who brings her fellow citizens to meet Jesus, to the women disciples who first tell of Jesus' resurrection.

These examples of women in the New Testament give me great

encouragement in my own calling, reminding me that God gifts, calls, and uses women to serve the people of God by delivering the Word of God. If you are feeling called by God for vocational ministry service, then you follow in the lineage of these women before you.

We began with Joel 2:28–29. Now read Galatians 3:28. What spiritual reality do you find there for the female in Christ? What physical, present implications does being "in Christ" have for women? At the very least, we know women can prophesy, meaning we, too, can have a ministry of the Word.

Yet what about those places in Scripture where Paul seems to command that women remain silent in the church? Does that undo all we have discussed about God's calling of women to vocational or gospel ministry? Let's turn now to one of those texts in the next chapter.

God, meet me where I am and take me where you would have me be to the glory of your name. Amen.

REFLECTION QUESTIONS

1. What surprised you about Mary? Why is she significant?

2. Look at the women we surveyed in this chapter. What else can we learn about how God calls women to his service? Did I miss anything? Was anything surprising?

3. Did anything change regarding women in ministry from the Old Testament to the New? If so, what? Did you make any additional or different observations?

DISCUSSION QUESTIONS

1. How do you approach ministry in light of Joel 2:28–29 and Galatians 3:28? Do you see yourself as a co-worker with men in ministry?

2. What does ministry look like for you as a woman? Challenges? Words of encouragement?

3. Which woman in the New Testament do you relate to the most? How have you been encouraged by how God called and used women in Scripture?

PERSONAL EXERCISES

1. Describe how these New Testament women help and encourage you in ministry, particularly in male-dominated areas.

2. Mary was afraid of her calling. Write down and discuss with your mentor any fears or stumbling blocks in regard to your calling that you need God's help to overcome.

3. Study a woman in church history whom God used in ministry. Some examples are Perpetua (d. 203), Marcella (325–410), Paula (347–404), Argula von Grumbach (1492–1554), Katharina Schütz Zell (1497/8–1562), Anne Askew (1521–1546), Lottie Moon (1840–1912), and Suzanne de Dietrich (1891–1981).

MINISTRY SPOTLIGHT:

LYDIA WHITLEY

Lydia Whitley had an unusual call to ministry. Before she felt called to ministry, Lydia first felt called to go to seminary. While she was an undergraduate student at Samford University in Birmingham, Alabama, Lydia felt uncomfortable with some statements being made by the leadership in her college church, but she could not articulate why she disagreed and what she believed from Scripture. Simultaneously, Lydia was growing spiritually during her time at Samford and had developed a passion for God's Word.

As her passion and frustration grew, Lydia began to desire seminary. Yet she was a little hesitant to believe that this was the best next step, because she was an interior design major. She worried about switching career paths, giving up her passion for art and architecture, and being academically inadequate for rigorous theological study. Others around Lydia, especially her parents, saw the Lord's calling on her life and encouraged her to attend seminary. But perhaps the most unexpected encouragement to go to seminary came from one of her design professors.

"He said to me, 'Lydia, we had this exact same conversation a year ago. I think seminary is your answer.' God placed that desire in my heart, which had not faded but had only grown stronger," she said.

Lydia was accepted to Beeson Divinity School. Initially, she went to seminary for personal spiritual formation, but during her time there, the Lord opened her eyes to a need for more theologically trained women serving in the church. While she was in seminary, Lydia and her husband, Taylor, went to London to do cross-cultural ministry. During their time in London, the Lord showed them the need for theologically trained ministers to serve in international churches.

"We knew that English-speaking congregations existed all over the world and believed their importance would continue to grow in our globalized economy as all tribes, tongues, and nations flock toward major global cities," Lydia said.

After Lydia graduated with her MDiv, the Lord led her and Taylor to the International Baptist Church in Stuttgart, Germany. Taylor is the youth minister and Lydia is the adult discipleship coordinator. In her position, Lydia organizes the church's small groups, which include the adult Sunday school classes and home groups. She works with men's, women's, and young adult ministries to provide Bible study curriculum, teacher training, retreats, and other discipleship events. She also has opportunities to teach, mentor, and speak at nearby churches.

Lydia finds joy in being able to serve alongside her husband, and says Priscilla and Aquila are their ministry role models. "Scripture only contains a few verses about them, yet it is obvious they were a strong husband-wife ministry team actively involved in the early church," Lydia said. "Serving together as wife and husband is much more a blessing than a challenge."

When I asked her what word of wisdom she would give to you, Lydia said, "Seek clarity and confirmation about your calling through prayer, reading God's Word, and talking to people you trust spiritually—but don't wait too long! As my wise design professor told me, if you consistently experience a desire to serve the Lord in a specific way or to receive theological training, then that is your answer. Now go for it!"

Since her ministry calling began progressively, Lydia will not be surprised if it continues to evolve. But she's not worried about what her ministry will look like or where she will be in five or ten years. Her trust is in the Lord, who goes before her and prepares the way.

CHAPTER 5

Does the Bible Restrict the Callings of Women?

A Closer Look at 1 Timothy 2:11–15

As a freshman in college, I sat in the office of the only female professor at the Pruet School of Christian Studies, the person who would later become my mentor. I timidly told her about my calling and that I thought it meant I could only be a pastor's wife. Now, being a pastor's wife is a noble calling. My mom is a pastor's wife, and I have the utmost respect for her and that role. Since I could not reconcile my own call to teach God's Word with 1 Timothy 2:11–15, the only possibility for me, I thought, was to get as close to formal ministry as possible by being a pastor's wife myself. At the time, I understood 1 Timothy to say that a ministry of proclamation was off-limits for me as a woman.

Up to this point in the book, I have made a case from Scripture that God calls, involves, and uses both men and women to accomplish his purpose on his behalf for the people of God, delivering the Word of God. However, many young women stop or are stumped when they arrive at 1 Timothy 2:11–15. For them, this passage is an obstacle in following God's call to a ministry calling that involves communicating the Word of God, especially through teaching or preaching. Many faithful believers and pastors teach—and believe—that a ministry of the Word is reserved only for men, and women are relegated to other, perhaps lesser ministries. Perhaps you can relate. In this chapter, I want to look at this passage head-on. Does this text stand in the way of pursuing a call to minister God's Word? Does it invalidate what we've concluded thus far about how God calls and uses women?

First Timothy 2:11–15 seems to restrict women from preaching and teaching with authority in the church. But before we examine it, let's remember that this passage is the inspired Word of God. We don't want to ignore these verses, minimize them, or write them off as irrelevant. At the same time, we must be careful not to give these verses veto power over the rest of what Scripture teaches. Instead, we want to put Scripture in conversation with itself as we work through these questions.

Let's pause here and read 1 Timothy 2:11–15:

> A woman should learn in quietness and full submission. I do not permit a woman to teach or to assume authority over a man; she must be quiet. For Adam was formed first, then Eve. And Adam was not the one deceived; it was the woman who was deceived and became a sinner. But women will be saved through childbearing—if they continue in faith, love and holiness with propriety.

For context, I would encourage you to read all of 1 Timothy 2. As you read, I want you to write down observations and questions you have regarding this passage.

It's important that we understand how the church has historically recognized its set of beliefs. On one hand, we have primary doctrines—those things that make us Christian, our core beliefs—that are non-negotiable to the faith. These are teachings summarized in the Apostles' Creed and the Nicene Creed, doctrines like the being of God (God as Father, Son, and Holy Spirit) and the means of our salvation. On the other hand, we have secondary doctrines. These are doctrines that do not directly affect our salvation and over which Christians historically have agreed to disagree, such as baptism, the nature of the Lord's Supper, and the end times. The discussion of the role of women in the church falls into these secondary doctrines, which means we can disagree on this issue and not compromise our Christian faith. It's something we can agree to disagree on. Isn't that a relief?

With that said, I want to say up front that in this chapter, I will *not* be advocating for the idea that being called to gospel ministry means all women should serve in ordained or pastoral ministry in a local church. I believe the answer to that question will depend on what gospel ministry means in your context, the tradition in which you belong, and your own sense of calling. Instead, what I want to demonstrate is that this passage does not negate the reality that God calls women—including you and me—to feed God's sheep. In some cases, that might only involve feeding other women and children, but the call is still valid and real, and we need to take it more seriously than we have in the past.

SETTING THE CONTEXT FOR THIS PASSAGE

Before we get into the meaning of the text, though, I want to set the context of 1 Timothy 2:11–15. First Timothy is a letter written by Paul to Timothy while Timothy is in Ephesus. Remember from chapter 2 of this book that Timothy is a missionary companion of Paul (Acts 16:1–5). He is like a son to Paul and is highly esteemed as his co-worker in the gospel.[1]

Paul leaves Timothy in Ephesus to help with the church he planted there. After leaving the Ephesian church elders in Miletus, Paul sails for Jerusalem, where he is later arrested (Acts 19:1–41 and 20:17–38). He writes 1 and 2 Timothy from prison, where he also writes the letter to Titus. Since it appears that he writes the letters at a similar time to deal with similar issues in the church, it is helpful to correlate these letters to each other.

Why does Paul leave Timothy in Ephesus?

So that you may command certain people not to teach false doctrines any longer or to devote themselves to myths and endless genealogies. Such things promote controversial speculations rather than advancing God's work—which is by faith. (1 Tim. 1:3b–4)

Another purpose statement is found in 1 Timothy 3:14–15:

I hope to come to you soon, but I am writing these things to you so that, if I delay, you may know how one ought to behave in the household of God, which is the church of the living God, a pillar and buttress of the truth. (ESV)

Paul ends the letter to Timothy similarly to how he begins it—by admonishing Timothy to guard himself from false teaching:

Timothy, guard what has been entrusted to your care. Turn away from godless chatter and the opposing ideas of what is falsely called knowledge, which some have professed and in so doing have departed from the faith. (6:20–21)

References to false teaching make up about 50 percent of the letter's contents, and false teaching and women compose 60 percent of the letter.[2] Paul says two church members have "shipwrecked their faith" and have been handed over to Satan (1 Tim. 1:20), some young widows have turned to follow Satan (1 Tim. 5:14–15), and even some elders have been rebuked (1 Tim. 5:20). Therefore, this is a letter of emergency meant to guide Timothy in how to immediately rectify a dangerous-to-the-gospel situation.

In addition to the immediate context of the book, it is also helpful to look at some of the broader historical context. As it relates to the directions to women in 1 Timothy 2:9–15, it might be helpful to look at the context of the ancient Roman wives and Roman widows. Evangelical scholar Bruce Winter has noted that around the period when 1 Timothy is written, there is a powerful movement among some women of the Roman Empire.[3] (Remember, Ephesus is a Roman city.) These "new women" have gone against traditional Roman morals by flaunting their bodies through expensive jewelry, elaborate hairdos, and unhealthy independence from their husbands. Winter argues that the sharp commands to women in 1 Timothy 2:9–15 and widows in 5:11–15 come as a result of this type of behavior entering the churches planted by Paul.[4] So Paul is not attacking women *as such*, but women who behave like these "new women."

One example of this is the similarities between what Paul says in verse 9 and what the Roman philosopher Seneca writes to his mother. Paul writes, "I also want the women to dress modestly, with decency and propriety, adorning themselves, not with elaborate hairstyles or gold or pearls or expensive clothes." Compare this now to Seneca:

> Unchastity, the greatest evil of our time, has never classed you with the great majority of women. Jewels have not moved you, nor pearls . . . You have never defiled your face with paints and cosmetics. Never have you fancied the kind of dress that exposed no greater nakedness by being removed. Your only ornament, the kind of beauty that time does not tarnish, is the great honour of modesty.[5]

Why would Paul instruct the Ephesian women this way if some of these "new" Roman values had not entered through the church doors? Winter argues that the reason the women must be silent and not teach is because the behavior of the women in the church in Ephesus mirrors the behavior of these "new" Roman women. This is a likely factor, but perhaps it is not the only reason Paul speaks the way he does.

TWO FRAMEWORKS FOR INTERPRETATION

We should use the two frameworks Paul uses as we work through our passage. The first framework is the advancement of the gospel.

Framework 1: The Gospel

Paul's main concern, as it always is in his letters and mission, is the gospel of Jesus Christ that saves. His concern is for the people's salvation. In 1 Timothy 1:3–4, Paul commands Timothy to stay in Ephesus and commands certain people not to teach false doctrines so that God's work might advance. God wants all people to be saved and to come to a knowledge of the truth. This is articulated in 1 Timothy 2:4–6. Paul writes, "For there is one God and one mediator between God and mankind, the man Christ Jesus, who gave himself as a ransom for all people." Paul makes this point again, in 4:10–11, saying, "That is why we labor and strive, because we have put our hope in the living God, who is the Savior of all people, and especially of those who believe. Command and teach these things." For Paul, to be concerned about the gospel going forth unhindered means he must be equally concerned with those people and those doctrines that oppose the gospel and want to stop it. Paul will do whatever it takes to stop false teaching.

Framework 2: The Church

The second framework is Paul's vision for the church. Paul envisions a church where both men and women are active in worship together, serving side by side. Paul begins 1 Timothy 2 with instructions for when the church gathers. His first instruction is that the church pray for all people. Paul envisions both men and women praying (1 Cor. 11). In 1 Timothy 2:8, Paul tells the men to pray instead of disputing with one another, and not to pray with anger in their hearts. In Greek, verse 9 begins "Likewise the women . . ." Likewise the women (when they pray) should dress modestly and humbly. Prayer is a central part of worship and is part of what the church does when it gathers. Paul, like a good pastor, is trying to correct some issues in this church. No doubt today, both instructions cross-apply to both genders. Women also should not pray with anger in their hearts or while they are in dispute, and likewise men should dress modestly and humbly.[6]

One of the most fascinating and eye-opening experiences during my trip to Israel was when we went to the Western Wall in Jerusalem on Friday night, the beginning of the Jews' Shabbat (Sabbath). Men and women couldn't pray together, so we were separated by a dividing wall. What Jesus does in accepting women to be his disciples and involving them in his ministry is almost unheard of, perhaps even somewhat radical. He tears down the wall, spiritually speaking, that divides men and women in prayer. Paul's vision of men and women worshipping and praying together isn't something new but is something he received from Jesus himself. What is true in Jesus' and Paul's time is also true now.

Later in 1 Timothy 2, Paul references Genesis and the first human couple. The Genesis account brings to mind a time prior to Adam and Eve's deception, a time when they were serving and worshipping side by side. Do you remember our discussion in chapter 1? The garden was like a temple of the living God, where God dwelt with man and woman, and in a way, Adam and Eve were priests in that temple, serving and worshipping the Lord God side by side. Both man and woman reflect the image of God in a unique way, and both genders are needed to display the full image of God. The first "church" (Adam and Eve) and the New Testament church should mirror each other, Paul would likely say. We see this today in our own churches: men and women worshipping, praying, and serving together.

Perhaps even more important is the church's reputation in society. If the church's witness is tarnished in society, how will people outside the church hear and accept the gospel of Jesus Christ? If Paul's primary concern is the gospel that saves, and the church is the caretaker of and witness to it, then the church's witness must be of vital importance so as not to compromise its mission to deliver the gospel. If the "new" Roman women's values are upsetting the culture and society (Seneca) and if these values are entering the church, then its witness in society will be compromised.

WHAT DOES 1 TIMOTHY 2:11–15 MEAN?

Now we get to the fun, difficult work of interpreting our passage. Interpreting this passage isn't impossible, for we believe that the Spirit is at work in God's Word and in us, but it does require careful study. Let's get to it!

Verse 11: Be a Humble Learner

A woman should learn in quietness and full submission.

1 TIMOTHY 2:11

The key takeaway from verse 11 is simple but profound: Paul desires women to be humble learners of the gospel. Paul begins our passage with, "A woman should learn . . ." Broadly speaking, in our western culture, women learning is widely accepted. Both males and females are given equal opportunities to learn at every level both outside and inside the church. But this hasn't always been the case, even in our own country. It wasn't until the 1900s, specifically from the 1930s to the 1950s, that women were admitted—and welcomed—to colleges in large numbers. In biblical times, and in the Jewish culture of those times, girls were not expected and not always allowed to learn in the same way as boys. With a few exceptions, all disciples of rabbis were male.

Jesus changes this by allowing—even inviting—women to take the position of disciple. Consider Mary, who sits at the feet of Jesus learning from him while her sister Martha prepares a meal. Jesus tells Martha that Mary has chosen the good portion (Luke 10:38–42). In Luke 8 we read of women accompanying Jesus and numbering among the larger number of disciples outside of the Twelve. Echoing Jesus' ministry, Paul says positively, "Let a woman learn" (1 Tim. 2:11 ESV).

Why does Paul want women to learn? First, Paul writes in 1 Timothy 2:4 that God desires *all* to "come to a knowledge of the truth," that is, to be saved. As we have discussed, all believers are God's sheep—men *and* women, old *and* young. The gospel of Jesus Christ and Holy Scripture are for both men *and* women. Women are to learn because the message of hope is for them, too!

Second, learning the true gospel that saves is the best line of defense against false teaching. When Paul writes again in 2 Timothy, he describes a situation in which false teachers have swayed a certain group of "gullible" women to embrace a false gospel. Speaking of the false teachers, Paul writes, "They are the kind who worm their way into homes and gain control over *gullible* women, who are loaded down with sins and are swayed by all kinds of evil desires, *always learning but never able to come to a knowledge of the truth*" (2 Tim. 3:6–7, emphasis mine). In these verses, Paul is giving us a glimpse into *one kind* of woman in the church in Ephesus that he is addressing. The irony—and tragedy—is that they are "always learning but never able to come to a knowledge of the truth." They are learning, but they are not learning the true gospel that saves (1 Tim. 2:4; 2 Tim. 3:15). The reason these women can never come to a knowledge of the truth is because what they are learning opposes the truth![7] Therefore, it is plausible that Paul's instruction is also meant to keep women who are gullible from being won over by false teaching. Let women learn the truth, Paul says, and the truth will prevail over the false teaching.

Third, Paul envisions the women learning so that they can teach other women and presumably children, as Timothy's own mother and grandmother did with him (2 Tim. 1:5; 3:15). Titus 2:3–5 says, "Likewise, teach the older women to be reverent in the way they live, not to be slanderers or addicted to much wine, but to *teach* what is good. Then they can urge the younger women to love their husbands and children, to be self-controlled and pure, to be busy at home, to be kind, and to be subject to their husbands, so that no one will malign the word of God" (emphasis mine). "What is good" and right living should never be taught devoid of doctrine or the gospel of Jesus Christ as found in Scripture; otherwise the teaching risks being moralistic but not necessarily Christian. Thus, in applying Titus and 1 Timothy, we should view learning Scripture as a prerequisite for women who will be teaching "what is good" (which I hope includes doctrine!) to women and children. To be sure, not everyone who learns is given the gift of teaching or called to teach in formal gospel ministry, but everyone who teaches should first and foremost be a learner.

So far we've concluded that women should learn for their own knowledge, so they won't be led astray, and so they can teach the gospel to others. But *how* are we to learn? If women are to learn this knowledge of truth, Paul says, then we need to learn in quietness and submissiveness. This is what he is getting at in 1 Timothy 2:11. Have you ever tried teaching children? Half the battle of teaching children is getting them to be quiet and to listen. Can you learn if you are busy talking while the teacher teaches? Can you learn if you are constantly questioning the teacher and not submitting to his or her authority?

Submission is a word that may make us feel uncomfortable since sometimes, in our culture, submission can become abusive. But in Scripture, submission is used positively. The New Testament tells us that Jesus Christ, though he was God's Son, submitted to the will of the Father (Heb. 5:7; Phil. 2:5–11). As Jesus' disciples, we are to submit to one another, just as he did. Paul says we are to submit "to one another out of reverence for Christ" (Eph. 5:21). He gets more specific. Wives are to submit to husbands. Slaves are to submit to their masters. Children are to submit to their parents. Pupils are to submit to their teachers. Citizens are to submit to the authorities. When we submit, we take the posture of our Lord. Therefore, this text not only teaches that women should learn; it also teaches the humble posture we should take as students of Scripture.

So far we see that Paul envisions a church where men and women are both active in worship, where women are learning, and where women are teaching at least other women. But what about verse 12?

Verse 12: Don't Be Domineering

I do not permit a woman to teach or to assume authority over a man; she must be quiet.

1 TIMOTHY 2:12

Paul's positive command to let women learn is followed by a negative instruction for Timothy to implement in Ephesus. What is Paul getting at in verse 12, and why? What Paul says here can be interpreted a couple of ways.

The first interpretation says that this verse means women should not serve as elders or pastors-teachers, positions that would mean they are in authority over and/or teaching men.[8] This instruction is "permanently applicable" because it is grounded in creation arguments in verses 13 and 14,[9] which we will get to momentarily.

However, New Testament scholar Andreas Köstenberger says that nothing is said to keep women from ministering to women and children, participating in an advisory role in church leadership, or instructing men privately with their husbands.[10] He says, "The parallel 1 Pet. 3:4, which commends a 'gentle and quiet spirit,' hardly envisions women literally being silent at all times."[11]

A second interpretation says that given the grave situation in Ephesus, Paul is ordering the church in Ephesus in a way that resonates with the culture of that time and that pushes against the "new" Roman women's values. Paul wants to protect the witness or reputation of the church to protect the mission of the church to deliver the gospel. Therefore, those who hold to this interpretation say this prohibition should be understood as culturally bound and applicable during Paul's day but not necessarily in our day, depending on the context. New Testament scholar Philip Towner says,

> But in any case, in the end experimentation with greater freedom in women's ministry activities might, for the sake of the church's mission, need to move in concert with cultural trends. What this means for Christianity in traditional Asian or Muslim contexts is that too much too fast could endanger the church's witness and credibility. But in much of the Western world, too little too slow could neutralize the church's impact in society just as effectively.[12]

Where do these two interpretations leave us as women called to a ministry of the Word? For those of you who do not feel called to be in teaching or authoritative positions over men, you see that Köstenberger says you still have ministry opportunities. If you find yourself in traditions that ordain women as pastors or deacons, you will resonate with the second interpretation. But even then, following Towner's interpretation, if God is calling you to cultures where a woman in authority would compromise the church's mission, then consider serving in other ways. However, I want to encourage you, no matter your call or church tradition, to read scholars who offer different interpretations of these verses. Take on a posture of humility and submission, and *learn*. But before we move on to the next two verses, let's look a little closer at the Greek word *authentein*, which is translated in the NIV as "to assume authority," and what Paul means when he says a woman is to be quiet.

Authentein doesn't appear anywhere in the Greek New Testament except here.[13] For that reason, it is a difficult word to translate. In Paul's day, the verbal forms of this word are rare; the few examples we have are used within violent or negative contexts.[14] Given that most of the cases where this word is used, it is used negatively, given the context of the "new" Roman woman, and given the issue of false teaching, *authentein* is probably best understood negatively rather than as the more neutral "have authority." New Testament scholar I. Howard Marshall writes, "The issue seems rather to be the way in which one exercises the authority involved in teaching, the danger being that the women were acting in a way that threatened the men."[15] Many scholars, including Linda Belleville, Marshall, and Towner, translate this word as "domineering." New Testament scholar Philip Payne makes the following important comment about the sense of the word *authentein*: "Initiative, lack of delegation from above, is a common component in all the examples . . ."[16] Taking independent initiative and acting domineering is the exact opposite of humility and submission. This is especially important for women who adopt the second interpretation and find themselves in positions of authority in the church. Likewise, men are not to exercise this kind of "domineering" authority over women, which opposes godliness and holiness (1 Tim. 2:2) and the way Jesus himself served.

What about the instruction at the end of verse 12 that a woman is to remain quiet? Paul is not saying that women can never talk when the church meets, for in 1 Corinthians 11, he gives instructions for when women pray and prophesy in worship services. In 1 Corinthians 14:26, Paul says, "What then shall we say, brothers and sisters? When you come together, each of you has a hymn, or a word of instruction, a revelation, a tongue or an interpretation. Everything must be done so that the church may be built up." So instead of reading this verse (and this passage!) as Paul restricting women from gospel ministry within the church, understand this verse as Paul reiterating the kind of posture women should take *to learn*. Marshall says this verse is not prohibiting women from all speech in church meeting, but rather "the limited reference here is to speaking out of turn and thereby interrupting the lesson."[17] The posture Paul describes is not gender-specific. Even though Paul is speaking directly about women here, *all disciples*—men and women—should learn and should do so in quietness and submission if they want to come to a knowledge of the truth (1 Cor. 16:16 and Gal. 6:6).[18]

Verses 13–14: An Illustration, Not a Norm

> For Adam was formed first, then Eve. And Adam was not the one deceived; it was the woman who was deceived and became a sinner.
>
> 1 TIMOTHY 2:13–14

Those who hold to the first interpretation of 1 Timothy 2:12 say that the prohibition given in verse 12 is grounded in the "divine order of creation"[19] outlined in verse 13—man was created first and woman second. Let's look closer at this interpretation.

Verse 13 is, positively speaking, the way in which the first "church" was ordered and therefore what the New Testament church (and we today) should copy. Why should women not teach or have authority over men? Or, positively speaking, why should men be in authority over women? Those who hold this interpretation say it is because that is how God ordered the first human couple and this ordering is good. Those who hold to this interpretation also say that the idea of being created first is the same as being firstborn, also called primogeniture. Primogeniture refers to the rights that come with being the firstborn. If you've ever watched the British TV series *Downton Abbey*, it may help you understand this. England had a law that ensured property was passed to the firstborn son; consecutive sons and daughters received no share of the estate. Primogeniture existed in the ancient world during the time of Scripture, too, but encompassed more than just land.

Verse 14, then, is what happens when that order is reversed, negatively speaking. This verse suggests that Eve was the "first target of deception."[20] The serpent's deception, Köstenberger and others say, comes through the reversal of roles. Satan deceives Eve, who then in turn deceives Adam,[21] thus illustrating what happens when the roles are reversed. Those who hold this interpretation place a strong emphasis on roles and ordering as the way to protect ourselves from being deceived.[22]

While verse 13 should be read literally, verse 14 is problematic if taken at face value. Köstenberger is quick—and right—to say that Paul is not claiming that Eve is more gullible than Adam or that Adam is never deceived or never becomes a sinner.[23] This verse also does not teach that women are more easily deceived simply because they are female. Scholar William J. Webb writes, "Women are not inherently (by virtue of their gender alone) more easily deceived than men . . . The degree to which one is deceivable or gullible is primarily related to factors such as age, experience, intelligence, education and personality."[24]

Now let's move to the second interpretation of these verses. Those who hold to the second interpretation of verse 12 given above view the prohibition in it as cultural and not universal (to be applied in all places and at all times), and say that verses 13–14 don't ground the prohibition but *illustrate* or show by analogy another time in salvation history when a woman was deceived. Let's look closer at this interpretation.

This interpretation says that these two verses should be seen as one illustration. Paul begins in verse 13 by summing up the Genesis 2 account of God creating the first human couple. Scholars who hold to both interpretations seem to agree that in this verse, Paul is giving a positive example from Scripture of men being in leadership over women based on creation order.[25] This interpretation holds that in verse 14, Paul is concerned with the nature of the fall, not the order of the fall. Like a good pastor, Paul is providing solutions supported by Scripture, as he always does. Webb says, "Eve fits well as an analogy or illustration of this problem at Ephesus."[26]

Support for reading these verses as illustrative is found in other letters wherein Paul uses the same examples from Adam and Eve to make a *different* application. In 1 Corinthians 11:8–9, Paul uses the same creation argument he uses in verse 13. In 1 Corinthians, Paul says that *because* Adam was formed first and then Eve, women should wear head coverings when they pray and prophesy. In the same way that head coverings are cultural, so is Paul's prohibition in verse 12, this interpretation says. Likewise, Paul uses the same argument about Eve's deception in verse 14 and 2 Corinthians 11:3 as an analogy to *all* those in the church who are being deceived. New Testament scholar Craig Keener says that Paul often argues by analogy, using Old Testament passages to relate to the present day.[27] The analogy in these verses, then, is pointing to another time when false teaching came through a woman and disastrous results followed. Therefore, Keener and others say we should read 2 Timothy 2:11–15 as a whole, as a pastoral solution for churches where false teaching and disruptive behavior is coming through women. They argue that this text should not be read as the norm by which every church should operate.

You might be wondering which interpretation is correct. I'll let you make that decision as you read more from scholars and work it out with your mentors and pastors. However, I want to make a couple of brief comments about these verses for you to keep in mind as you work it out.

At the beginning of the chapter, I said I want to put 1 Timothy 2 in conversation with the rest of Scripture. So how does the rest of Scripture help us to interpret these first four verses?

First, consider how often God flips or inverts the "firstborn" system, turning the "first is best" mentality on its head. Ishmael was Abraham's first son, but Isaac inherited the birthright because he was the son of God's promise. Esau was the firstborn son, but his twin Jacob stole his birthright and was still blessed by God, going on to father the twelve tribes of Israel. God chose Moses to lead his people, even though Aaron was older. David was the youngest of all his brothers but received the greatest inheritance.

Notice how often God inverts our human systems. In Matthew

20, Jesus says, "The last will be first, and the first will be last" (v. 16). God chooses the foolish things of this world to shame the wise (1 Cor. 1:25–27). He uses the weak to shame the strong (1 Cor. 1:27). He says the least will be the greatest (Luke 9:48) and that adults must become like children to inherit heaven (Matt. 18:2–4). God chooses Israel even though she is the fewest of all people (Deut. 7:7). God chooses the last born and the weaker brothers. God chooses a woman, Deborah, over a man to judge and lead Israel (Judg. 4–5). God chooses a young virgin named Mary in a country town to carry God's Son. God himself becomes a tiny, fragile baby born to parents of no significance, and one day God the Father will put everything under his feet and authority (Eph. 1:22). Even in the Pastoral Epistles, Paul has a young Timothy in charge of the church, including elders. This is why Paul tells Timothy not to let anyone look down on him because he is young and at the same time not to rebuke an older man harshly (1 Tim. 4:12; 5:1). God often chooses the weak, the young, the small, the last, and the least expected because (a) he loves us and (b) so that his power may be made known in a world that prizes the oldest, the biggest, the strongest, and the most powerful. For the wisdom and power of God is made known supremely on a cross. While it may seem like God is turning everything upside down, it is possible he is turning things right side up.

Second, we must be careful not to link order with false teaching as if a certain order is preventative of false teaching. In many cases today, false teaching is coming through a male pastor of a church. I imagine you can think of at least one example! Order is not a fail-safe against false teaching. False teaching enters the church through many doors. One of those doors is women's ministry, often because churches are not hiring called, *biblically learned* women to teach the women of the church. The best defense against false teaching is having God-called, trained ministers of the gospel on staff, including those who oversee women's and children's ministries.

Third, no matter our interpretation of 1 Timothy 2, we must still recognize that we sit at the feet of female teachers every time we approach the divinely inspired speech of women in Scripture.

We often say that we sit at the feet of Peter or Paul when we read their letters or sermons in the book of Acts, or at the feet of Moses when we read the first five books of the Old Testament. Likewise, Deborah, Huldah, Hannah, Mary, Elizabeth, and others have something to teach us today about God, his Word, and the working out of salvation in Jesus Christ because God has determined to reveal himself through their testimony.

Verse 15: A Holistic Calling

> But women will be saved through childbearing—if they continue in faith, love and holiness with propriety.
>
> 1 TIMOTHY 2:15

When we get to this last verse of our passage, our antennas go up, telling us something is not right with what we are reading. At face value, this verse seems to oppose the gospel story of Scripture that all are saved through the atoning work of Jesus Christ. So how are we supposed to understand what Paul is saying here? Let me begin with what Paul is *not* saying. He is not referring to our conversion. In Ephesians 2:8–10, Paul writes that no one can be saved by any work of their own apart from the work of Jesus Christ. This includes childbearing and childrearing! If this were the case, what would happen to single women and childless women? Let's briefly look at several explanations of what Paul probably means.

One possible interpretation of this verse hinges on how you translate what the NIV translates as "childbearing." Some scholars translate this word—because of a definite article that comes before it—as "the Childbirth." Thus, they say, this verse is a reference to the childbirth of Jesus that came through one woman, Mary. Therefore, Paul is saying women (and men) will be saved through the advent of Jesus Christ, a translation that fits with the gospel of Jesus Christ proclaimed throughout the rest of the New Testament.[28]

A second interpretation reads this verse as a way of Paul undoing the work of the false teaching. The content of the false teaching in Ephesus has an anti-material, anti-body tilt. In 1 Timothy 4:3,

Paul says, "They forbid people to marry and order them to abstain from certain foods." Unlike what they teach (that marriage and certain foods are bad), Paul says that everything God creates is good (v. 4). It is probable, given Paul's description of the false teaching and the "new" Roman women's morals, that women are forsaking their families, homes, and calling and possibly even aborting babies. In contrast to the false teachers, Paul is calling women to work out their salvation within their homes and vocations and to see these things as good. Towner writes, "Christian women were not to forego or avoid pregnancy. Willingness to become pregnant (and perhaps to see it through to childbirth) was apparently a very real concern."[29] The qualities listed at the end of verse 15—faith, love, and holiness—are marks or fruit of a true follower of Jesus Christ (Gal. 5:22–23). The whole of our existence should be characterized by faith, love, and holiness as a testimony to the work of Jesus Christ and the Holy Spirit in our lives.

For us today, this is a reminder that our calls to ministry should never justify neglecting the ministry of the home and family, even if it means that formal ministry is placed "on hold" for a little while. At the same time, Paul is not saying to single and childless females, you must marry and have children to experience the fullness of God's promises and the Christian life (1 Cor. 7:7–8). Rather, like the Roman women in the church in Ephesus, we face an idolatrous, selfish, and promiscuous culture that attacks the family, the self, and a Christian view of holiness. As Peter writes, "But just as he who called you is holy, so be holy in all you do" (1 Pet. 1:15).

WHAT DOES IT MEAN FOR US TODAY?

So now what? How do we apply this passage to the church today? First, we should see that Paul envisions a church where both men and women are active in worship and in prayer. This is a church where both men and women are serving side by side, displaying the glory of God, for the sake of the gospel. Paul envisions a church where all its members are learning in humility to gain the knowledge of God and so that they may in turn teach others. It's a church that is committed to the gospel, one where false teaching has no hold, one where its members are working out their salvation with fear and trembling in the vocations and places to which God has called them.

In Titus 2, Paul tells everyone in the church how they ought to behave: old men, young men, old women, and bondservants. At the very end of the section, Paul says they are to behave this way "so that in everything they may *adorn* the doctrine of God our Savior" (v. 10 ESV, emphasis mine). This is a helpful lens through which to look at our passage. The instructions to women in 1 Timothy 2 begin in verse 9 with instructions concerning physical adornment and end in verse 15 with character adornment. Paul's greatest concern is that we adorn the gospel of Jesus Christ, not ourselves.

What about these "new" Roman women? First, our historical and cultural context always bears weight. When you study any person in history, you will study what's going on in history that can help explain why that person said what she said and did what she did. No one lives in a historical or cultural vacuum, so we must recognize that something is going on in Ephesus and in this church that can help us better understand the situation, even though we aren't given all the details. Second, there is good evidence that there is a movement of these Roman women going against the Roman mores. Therefore, we should bear this historical context in mind as a possible or even likely bridge to understanding what Paul is saying and doing in this letter.

What does this mean for me, a woman called to ministry? First, this passage does *not* teach that God does *not* call women to ministry. This passage is not a treatise on women in ministry. Some may say— and you may conclude—that it does, at least, teach us what roles are restricted for women. Yet even then, Paul isn't necessarily restricting women from *all* ministry. He's very concerned with the situation at hand. If he is restricting women from all ministry, then why does he affirm women for their ministry in Romans 16 and elsewhere?

In addition, this passage teaches that women should and need to learn the gospel. It's important; it's imperative! The question for women who sense a call to ministry is this: Who is going to be equipped to teach other women? We should keep in mind that this passage is set within the context of the Pastoral Epistles, and as such, it teaches us that God calls women to teach, at the very least, other women and children.

When read carefully and in context, this passage should not be viewed as an obstacle to ministry. After working through this passage with a mentor, seeing the variety of possible interpretations freed me up to ask God to show me what ministry could look like within my church tradition. I no longer assumed being a pastor's wife was the *only* option available to me.

I want to reiterate again that what ministry looks like for you will largely depend on your church and denomination and the Lord Jesus' call on your life. As you seek to apply this passage to your situation, let me encourage you to prepare for ministry by spending time learning. Submit to those in authority over you. Live a life of holiness, humility, and modesty, showing respect to our brothers in ministry. Last, but not least, be concerned about the advancement of the gospel. The advancement of the gospel may look different depending on where you are, but like Paul, we should remember that the gospel teaches us to surrender our rights (1 Cor. 9:1–18) and do everything possible to make the name of Jesus known.

Jesus was concerned that the harvest was plentiful but the workers were few (Matt. 9:37–38). Paul, at the beginning of 1 Timothy 2, says that God desires all people to be saved. In Romans 10:14–15, Paul writes,

> How, then, can they call on the one they have not believed in? And how can they believe in the one of whom they have not heard? And how can they hear without someone preaching to them? And how can anyone preach unless they are sent? As it is written: "How beautiful are the feet of those who bring good news!"

You do not have to be a senior pastor or preach where men are present to have a call to Word-based ministry. Plenty of gospel ministry work needs doing among women, youth, and children. On the other hand, you may be in a denomination or church that ordains women and allows you greater freedom to pursue your calling as a woman in ministry. Wherever God has placed you, if he has called you to ministry, he will provide a way for you to serve. Just as God raised up Miriam, Deborah, Huldah, Mary, Priscilla, and other women for unique purposes in salvation history, delivering his word for the people of God, so God's plan for establishing his kingdom includes women. Work to counter false teaching. Teach other women the knowledge of truth. There's so much work to be done, and many have yet to hear the good news about Jesus. God desires workers because he wants the world to hear the excellent news and be saved. If God has called you to be a minister of the gospel of Jesus Christ, he will provide a place in the church for you to serve.

Victoria "Vickie" Gaston has been in ministry for many years, teaching spiritual formation classes and overseeing spiritual life ministries at a seminary. She says, "Women are sometimes reticent to step forward and follow the call of Christ into ministry. It is my hope we all recognize and trust our loving heavenly Father and faithfully understand that to answer the call of Christ is to follow, without apology, his loving lead, no matter where and in what role in ministry he gives us the privilege of serving him."

> "Breathe in me, O Holy Spirit,
> That my thoughts may all be holy.
> Act in me, O Holy Spirit,
> That my work, too, may be holy.
> Draw my heart, O Holy Spirit,
> That I love but what is holy.
> Strengthen me, O Holy Spirit,
> To defend all that is holy.
> Guard me, then, O Holy Spirit,
> That I always may be holy."
>
> AUGUSTINE[30]

REFLECTION QUESTIONS

1. I began this chapter saying that for me, this passage was an obstacle to ministry when I was a freshman in college. Has this passage been an obstacle for you? If so, why? Write out how you understood the passage before and the questions it raised for you. Now, in light of this chapter, is it less of an obstacle? Did this chapter raise other questions for you? If so, what are they? Do you feel confused or comforted? Journal your response.

2. Many scholars believe that our passage, read in light of all of 1 Timothy, 2 Timothy, and Titus, teaches that women are to learn, in part and at least, to teach other women. How does this viewpoint encourage you in your own call?

3. What kind of attitude does this passage prompt us to have? Read this passage in light of these Scriptures: Ephesians 5:21, Philippians 2:1–18, Colossians 3:12, and 1 Peter 5:5. What kind of attitude should Christians have? Now write out or think of ways this attitude is important in ministry contexts.

DISCUSSION POINTS

1. What do you understand to be the meaning of this passage? Work out questions, explanations, and applications with your mentor. Read commentaries and books on this passage together.

2. What would application of this passage to your ministry look like?

PERSONAL EXERCISES

1. Read what other people have to say about this passage and on the topic of women in ministry. This chapter is only a brief introduction to or summary of what scholars are saying.

2. Read 1 Corinthians 14:34–35, another passage that seems to restrict women from some ministry areas, in different translations. Write out observations or questions you have. Does this chapter shed any light on any of this passage? If so, how?

MINISTRY SPOTLIGHT:

TISH HARRISON WARREN

Tish Harrison Warren was thirteen or fourteen when she sensed a possible call to ministry. But there was no clear, systematic road map available to show her how women could enter vocational ministry. So early on, she interpreted this call to mean she needed to serve in a lay capacity or as a missionary.

Reflecting on this initial calling, Tish said, "I felt like men have clear steps about how to enter the vocation of ministry. It felt like I was kind of in the bush with a machete, slowly slashing through tall grass and thickets, making a trail to serve in the church, with very little idea of what I was doing or how this would look in the end."

She waited until she was a senior in high school to publicly tell her church family that she was called to vocational ministry. A few people told her afterward, "We are so glad you are going into ministry. You will make such a great pastor's wife."

During the next eight years, Tish tried to make sense of her calling by involving herself in different ministries and learning experiences. For example, she served as a staff intern at her church, taught English overseas for a summer, worked with homeless teenagers, and worked in a drug rehab facility for teens. Tish eventually married a lawyer. During this time, she took a seminary class at night and loved it. Not long after, she and her husband decided to go to seminary together, so they moved to South Hamilton, Massachusetts, to attend Gordon-Conwell Theological Seminary.

Tish loved her time in seminary learning theology, church history, Greek, and the rest. Seminary also gave her a lens through which to see the world theologically.

After seminary, Tish and her husband became Anglicans. For the first time in her life, ordination was a possibility, and she had to discern if it was the path of ministry to which God was directing her. At first she was unsure and full of doubt, but she eventually entered a five-year-long ordination process. Her husband, too, began the ordination process, and they were ordained to the priesthood on the same day. Ironically, she says, she did become a pastor's wife after all, but she also became a pastor herself.

As she was going through the ordination process after seminary, Tish worked with InterVarsity Graduate and Faculty Ministries (IV GFM) at Vanderbilt University in Nashville, Tennessee, for four years. She also began ministering through writing. After her ordination as a transitional deacon, she and her husband moved to Austin, Texas, where she continued working with IV GFM at the University of Texas.

It was in Austin that Tish's writing career really picked up. She began writing regularly for *Christianity Today, Her.meneutics,* and *The Well,* and published her first book, *Liturgy of the Ordinary.*

What does ministry look like for Tish today? She and her husband now live in Pittsburgh, Pennsylvania, where they are both associate rectors at the Church of the Ascension. In this role, Tish oversees congregational care and the prayer ministry, works with "emerging adults" (twentysomethings), preaches, and has other pastoral duties. She also continues trying to juggle writing, priesthood, and motherhood.

When I asked her what she would say to you, she said, "It's important that you don't go into ministry to make some kind of statement about women in ministry (that we can do this). Only go into ministry if you love people and serving the church and the gospel and (mostly) if you sense a call to ministry that's been affirmed by close friends and community. There is a great need for women to be in ministry, especially women who really love the church. No one—male or female—has a right to be in ministry or to be ordained or to be used by God, so be humble. We are all completely dispensable. But if this may be your calling, ask the Lord to send harvesters into the field, because women desperately need other trained and theologically rooted women who are spiritual authorities in their lives and in the church. I see an enormous hunger from women (and men) for female leaders they can trust."

CHAPTER 6

What Are Spiritual Gifts?

Some of you may feel confident in God's call on your life. But even if you are, you may still wrestle with some of the details. *What will this ministry look like? Where will I exercise my call? Will I be delivering the Word of God through preaching, teaching, or writing? Will this ministry take place within the church on a staff or elsewhere, perhaps on a college campus, in a Bible translating organization, in a hospital as a chaplain, or in a university or seminary teaching the Bible? How do I fully embrace what God has gifted me to do?*

I struggled with these questions for many years. Sadly, most of my youth and college ministers didn't know how to help me answer them. They tried giving me spiritual gifts tests, but I was typically left to myself to figure out what my gifts were and how to use them to serve the body of Christ. In this chapter, I want to help you begin answering these questions by taking a closer look at the topic of spiritual gifts. Paul says God gives spiritual gifts to those who are called by him for the purpose of equipping the body of believers. This includes those who are gifted to care for the people of God by delivering the Word of God. If God is calling you to this type of ministry, then what gifts might he give you?

One text from Scripture that helps us answer this question is Ephesians 4:11–13:

> So Christ himself gave the apostles, the prophets, the evangelists, the pastors and teachers, to equip his people for works of service, so that the body of Christ may be built up until we all reach unity in the faith and in the knowledge of the Son of God and become mature, attaining to the whole measure of the fullness of Christ.

Let's look at these verses together in light of what we have studied in Scripture thus far, and then ask ourselves this question: *How is God gifting us for the call he has given us?*

JESUS CHRIST, THE GIVER OF GIFTS

Everything—our salvation, calling, and spiritual gifts—begins and ends with Jesus. Jesus, with the Father and Spirit, is the alpha and omega and the One to whom all glory is given. Paul speaks of these gifts in Ephesians 4:11 as existing *in* Jesus Christ. Lest we begin to think more highly of ourselves or that we can muster up the skills needed for the call of our own will, Paul reminds us that Jesus is the origin and the orchestrator. It is Jesus who calls people into his service. Christ gives the gifts that enable people to be apostles, prophets, evangelists, and more, and he gives these people to the church, his body. *Christ* gives who he needs to build up *Christ's* body so that the people of God might come to faith and knowledge in *Christ* and mature to the fullness of *Christ*. In Ephesians 4:11–13, Christ is mentioned four times! Jesus will ensure his own body is built and his purposes are fulfilled by raising up individuals to serve in these ways.

As I've already said, God will not leave the shepherding of his church and the spreading of his mission to "chance," to whomever aspires to it or volunteers. No. The story of Scripture and these verses tell us something different: that God is actively calling, actively setting apart people to do this kind of work. Jesus Christ did not come to this earth, die, and rise again to reconcile people to God only to withdraw and not be involved with his church.

It is Jesus Christ who gives ministers to his people. The Greek is emphatic—Christ *himself.* This is still true today. We are called by Christ, gifted by Christ, for the building up of the people of Christ. Let that truth sink into your heart. A true Christian ministry will be Christ-centered and Christ-glorifying, because the call ultimately comes from Jesus Christ.

Grace-Given Gifts

Who are these people in Ephesians 4:11—the apostles, the prophets, the evangelists, the pastors and teachers? The roles they fill are a result of the spiritual gifts God has given them. Apostles have the gift of apostleship, prophets have the gift of prophecy, and so on. This can be confusing for us today because churches create positions that often require many gifts, and you apply to that position hoping your gifts will be a good fit, not the other way around.

We saw in Scripture that although Peter and Paul may have been known as apostles, they exercised many gifts and were also preachers, teachers, and more. But before we get too focused on the gifts themselves, let's look at what is behind the gifts. Paul reminds us that the reason we have spiritual gifts at all is because of God's grace towards us. He writes, "But to each one of us grace has been given as Christ apportioned it" (Eph. 4:7). Spiritual gifts, therefore, are God's grace-given gifts to us. It sounds a little redundant, doesn't it? Gifts are, by default, *given*. Also by default, gifts are not predicated on us deserving or earning them. Rather, gifts exist because of the grace of the giver. Paul also says this in Romans 12:6: "We have different gifts, *according to the grace* given to each of us" (emphasis mine).

The call to ministry came to Vickie Gaston when she was a teenager. But because of some traumatic experiences, Vickie became a "prodigal child." For many years she was in a spiritual wilderness, running from God, but his call never left her heart. After coming back to the Lord as an adult, she continued to deny the call because she felt unworthy of it. The Lord had other plans. She experienced the grace of Jesus, not just in the forgiveness of her sins but in the spiritual gifts that equipped her for the call she had received years before.

Gifts are deemed "spiritual" because they are given through the agency of the Holy Spirit. It's a designation of who they come from and who gives the power to the gift. Gifts do not reflect anything special about *us*. They are given only by God, according to his grace. This means we cannot manufacture or manipulate these gifts. If God has called us to equip believers, then he will qualify us by giving us the gifts we need. Remember, Moses was slow of speech and tongue, yet God gifted him for the task he was called to despite his lack of skills. We come to God with open hands and hearts, asking him to give us what we do not deserve but what he desires to give.

All of God's children are given gifts to use in his body (1 Cor. 12), but the ones mentioned here are of particular importance to our discussion of gospel ministry as we have been defining it in this book: called by God to deliver the Word of God to the people of God. The gifts mentioned here all have something in common: they all include a ministry of the Word of God. Let's look at each one.

APOSTLES

Apostle was a designation used for the twelve disciples and Paul, who had seen the resurrected Jesus and been commissioned by him to establish his church.[1] Others who did not possess quite the same authority as the Twelve were called apostles as well. The ones we know of include Silas (Acts 15:22), Timothy (1 Thess. 2:6–7), Apollos (1 Cor. 4:6–9), and Andronicus and Junia (Rom. 16:7). Remember, Christianity was in its infancy here. Apostles were instrumental in grounding the church in the authoritative teaching of Jesus Christ. We call their teaching *apostolic* teaching, which is accepted as the authoritative Word of God today. It is also accepted that the gift of apostleship ended with the early church (after the New Testament period). We wouldn't call anyone an apostle today. However, I see a great similarity between the work apostles were called to do and the work of church planters or missionaries. This should not surprise us, because the apostles carried out their ministries in the context of church planting and missions. God is still in the business of raising up missionaries to take the apostolic teaching found in the New Testament to people who have never heard of Jesus and to establish new churches in those lands.

PROPHETS

When I was growing up, prophecy was a gift I never really understood. It was old, foreign, *other*. Like apostleship, I assumed prophecy stopped with the close of Scripture. But does it? You may remember from the first part of the book that many of the people we studied had the gift of prophecy. As a refresher, who were prophets? Moses, himself a prophet, tells the people:

> The LORD your God will raise up for you a prophet like me from among you, from your fellow Israelites. You must listen to him. For this is what you asked of the LORD your God at Horeb on the day of the assembly when you said, "Let us not hear the voice of the LORD our God nor see this great fire anymore, or we will die." The LORD said to me: "What they say is good. I will raise up for them a prophet like you from among their fellow Israelites, and *I will put my words in his mouth. He will tell them everything I command him...* You may say to yourselves, "How can we know when a message has not been spoken by the LORD?" If what a prophet proclaims in the name of the LORD does not take place or come true, that is a message the LORD has not spoken. That prophet has spoken presumptuously, so do not be alarmed. (Deut. 18:15–18, 21–22, emphasis mine)

In the Old Testament, prophets spoke the authoritative word of God to God's people. Much of what we have in the Old and New Testaments are inspired words given specifically through prophets. Prophets spoke messages that had a past, present, and future purpose. What does this mean? Sometimes we tend to think of prophets only as those who predicted the future. Indeed, they did speak of the future, as directed by God, whether it was a future of doom and judgment or a future of hope and salvation. But prophets also spoke messages that had a present situation in mind. They often urged the people to repent and turn to the Lord to escape impending judgment (Jonah). Thus, some scholars have said that the prophets did more forthtelling than foretelling. What may be most surprising, though, is that Old Testament prophets also gave messages about the past. They often reminded the people how God acted in the past, what God had already said, and, through the Holy

Spirit, interpreted the Law for the people (2 Kings 22:13).[2] In summary, Old Testament prophets were "vehicles" and "proclaimers" of the very word of God.[3]

In the New Testament, the gift of prophecy continues, but is it the same? Twice in Ephesians, prophets are grouped together with apostles. In Ephesians 2:19–20 Paul writes, "Consequently, you are no longer foreigners and strangers, but fellow citizens with God's people and also members of his household, *built on the foundation of the apostles and prophets*, with Christ Jesus himself as the chief cornerstone" (emphasis mine). Frank Thielman writes that "apostles and prophets together form the foundation of the new multiethnic people of God (Eph. 2:20), a position that belongs to them because of their critical role in taking the gospel to the Gentiles (Eph. 3:5)."[4]

Interestingly, for the purposes of this book (as we mentioned in chapter 5), it is clear that in the New Testament church, women prophesied. Consider the following text from 1 Corinthians 11:5: "but every woman who prays or prophesies with her head uncovered . . ." Here, Paul goes on to instruct the woman who prophesies about the right attitude she is to adopt. What this passage makes clear, though, is that women *did* prophesy in the church, and that it was acceptable as long as it was done with the right attitude (1 Cor. 12:10, 27–30; 14:26–40). As scholar Gordon Fee has explained, prophesying meant exhorting the people of God on the basis of the Word of God.[5]

Argula von Grumbach was a woman who lived during the sixteenth century in Germany and who became actively involved in the Protestant Reformation. She is best known for the public letter she wrote to the Catholic leaders of the University of Ingolstadt, who had persecuted a young student for his Protestant faith. I mention her because she is an example of a woman who had the gift of prophecy (exhorting the people of God on the basis of the Word of God). She writes phrases like, "I cry out with the prophet Jeremiah," and spends the majority of her letter quoting and applying the message of the prophets to these leaders and to the present-day situation.

As we've already discussed, a sign of the new age of the Holy

Spirit was that men and women would prophesy (Joel 2:28–29; Acts 2:16–18). We are told many prophets were in Jerusalem: Agabus (Acts 11:28, 21:10), Philip's four daughters (Acts 21:8–9), and Judas and Silas (Acts 15:32). Also, as we saw above, Paul gives the impression that people prophesied in every church (1 Cor. 12–14; Eph. 2:20; 1 Tim. 4:14).

How did prophets function in the New Testament? We hinted at an answer above, but now let's go deeper. First, they spoke prophecy that was evangelistic. In Joel's prophecy, which Peter repeats and explains in Acts 2, prophecy is tied to salvation. In the days that God pours out his Spirit, "it shall come to pass that everyone who calls on the name of the LORD shall be saved" (Joel 2:32 ESV). We see this purpose of prophecy clearly laid out by Paul in 1 Corinthians 14:24–25:

> But if an unbeliever or an inquirer comes in while everyone is prophesying, they are convicted of sin and are brought under judgment by all, as the secrets of their hearts are laid bare. So they will fall down and worship God, exclaiming, "God is really among you!"

Prophecy that comes from God is designed to lead to worship of God. We see this even in Revelation—a book of prophecy—when the messenger tells John in chapter 19 verse 10, "'Worship God.' Why? "'For it is the Spirit of *prophecy* who bears testimony to Jesus.'" Prophecy points to the testimony of Jesus, and thereby results in worship of Jesus.

Second, prophecy sometimes consists of instruction. Paul explains the purpose of prophecy in 1 Corinthians 14 within the context of instruction (vv. 5–6, 12, 19). He ends the chapter by concluding, "For you can all prophesy in turn so that everyone may be instructed and encouraged" (1 Cor. 14:31).

In addition to prophecy being evangelistic and instructive, it is meant to be encouraging, as Paul says in 1 Corinthians 14:31. In fact, he begins chapter 14 by saying, "But the one who prophesies speaks to people for their *strengthening, encouraging and comfort*" (v. 3). We see this worked out in Acts 15:32: "Judas and Silas, who themselves were prophets, said much to encourage and strengthen the believers."

Finally, like the prophets of old, at least one prophet in the New Testament of whom we know, Agabus, also spoke of the future (Acts 11:27–30; 21:8–14).

So does God, through his Spirit, still give us the gift of prophecy today? The answer is yes. Let me qualify this answer by clarifying this, though. It's important to see that Paul elevated prophecy above all the spiritual gifts except apostleship. In 1 Corinthians 12:28–31, Paul lists prophets as second behind apostles. We've already seen how he grouped apostles and prophets as those who lay the foundation of Christ in the church in Ephesians 2:20. In 1 Corinthians 14, Paul spends the whole chapter comparing prophecy to speaking in tongues and says of all the gifts, "Follow the way of love and eagerly desire gifts of the Spirit, especially prophecy" (v. 1). In 1 Thessalonians 5:19–21, Paul writes, "Do not quench the Spirit. Do not treat prophecies with contempt but test them all." Paul's words should cause us to pause before dismissing prophecy.

Prophecy was a gift of the Spirit in both testaments and a sure sign of the coming age of the Holy Spirit as seen in Joel and Acts. If we have the same Spirit today as we have had for all time, then we should gladly accept that God gifts both men and women to prophesy. However, we should add that prophecy today does not include new revelation. We do well to heed the warning in Revelation 22:18–19,

> I warn everyone who hears the words of the prophecy of this scroll: If anyone adds anything to them, God will add to that person the plagues described in this scroll. And if anyone takes words away from this scroll of prophecy, God will take away from that person any share in the tree of life and in the Holy City, which are described in this scroll.

The inspired, revelatory Word of God is closed with the New Testament. Paul tells us to test prophecies in 1 Thessalonians, and all prophecy today must be tested against Scripture. Any prophecy that contradicts, adds to, or takes away from Scripture is not prophecy from God.

So what does prophecy look like today? Prophecy points to Jesus and his revealed Word. Go back and reread Revelation 19:10. The Spirit of prophecy bears testimony to Jesus. Today, prophecy, just as we find in Scripture, is meant to be evangelistic, instructive, and encouraging. In fact, prophecy is part of the gifting "package" that is given to those who are preachers and teachers of the Word. Grounded in Holy Scripture and prayer, the gift of prophecy is expressed by men and women when they exhort, convict, encourage, and give wisdom. This might occur in a home Bible study, a Sunday homily, or even in a one-to-one explanation of the Bible, for example.

EVANGELISTS

Evangelists are people who bring good news. The Greek word *evangelist* has the Greek root for "good news" within it. An evangelist, therefore, is someone who brings or proclaims good news. Used within the New Testament, the good news is the gospel of Jesus Christ. Only two people are given the designation of evangelist in the New Testament: Philip (Acts 21:8) and Timothy (2 Timothy 4:5). Philip is one of seven chosen in Acts 6:1–7 to help take care of the needs of the widows in the churches, but he also has a ministry of the gospel. Before we are told Philip is an evangelist, Luke narrates the proof of his evangelism ministry. In Acts 8:5, Luke writes, "Philip went down to a city in Samaria and proclaimed the Messiah there," and then later, "But when they believed Philip as he proclaimed the good news of the kingdom of God and the name of Jesus Christ, they were baptized, both men and women" (Acts 8:12). Philip is perhaps best known for preaching the gospel to the Ethiopian eunuch in Acts 8:

Then Philip ran up to the chariot and heard the man reading
Isaiah the prophet. "Do you understand what you are reading?"
Philip asked. "How can I," he said, "unless someone explains it to
me?" So he invited Philip to come up and sit with him . . . Then
Philip began with that very passage of Scripture and told him the
good news about Jesus. (vv. 30–31, 35)

Evangelists are best understood in Scripture as those who
travel to various places bringing the good news of Jesus Christ.[6]
Frank Thielman says, "Paul, then, probably thinks of 'evangelists,'
as similar to apostles but without their authority because of their
lack of direct connection to the historical Jesus. The evangelists
proclaim the message to which the apostles have been eye- and
earwitnesses."[7]

Evangelism is very much a part of who we are today. In fact, we
are called evangelicals, which shows how central it is to preach the
good news of Jesus Christ! Evangelists are those whose main vocation is to share the gospel with non-Christians, usually through
preaching and teaching.

Let's think of some people who are evangelists today or in
recent history. The first person who comes to mind is Billy Graham.
In fact, at one of his crusades in Little Rock, Arkansas in 1989, I first
heard the gospel articulated in a way that warmed my six-year-old
heart and led to my conversion. Others besides Billy Graham are
known for their evangelism ministry, including Anne Graham Lotz,
Ravi Zacharias, and Tim Keller. In chapter 2, I introduced you to
Cokiesha Bailey Robinson, who has an itinerant evangelism ministry. Perhaps you grew up in a church that had traveling evangelists
come through a few times a year.

But not all who have the gift of evangelism practice it as traveling evangelists. Evangelism is a gift that can be used in many
ministerial roles and with the accompaniment of other gifts. Going
back to Scripture, even though only two people are called evangelists, many others practiced the gift of evangelism alongside other
gifts. For example, Paul is an evangelist, proclaiming the good news

of Jesus Christ, even though that term is never used to describe him. Likewise, today you can find several ministers on my church staff who have the gift of evangelism and practice it within their preaching ministries. The chaplain of my son's private Christian school has the gift of evangelism and uses the gift in his work at the school almost daily. One of my professors from seminary has the gift of evangelism. The gift is evident whether he is teaching in the classroom or shopping in the grocery store. I mentioned Tim Keller, who has the gift of evangelism, which is often practiced within the context of his preaching and writing.

PASTOR-SHEPHERDS

Paul names pastors after evangelists. The word translated as "pastor" is actually the Greek word for "shepherd." It's fitting, isn't it, that Paul includes shepherds in this list. For we have seen that the gift of shepherding is a prominent gift given to many of those God calls in Scripture. After Jesus' ascension, shepherd was used as a metaphor for pastoring people, imitating the Great Shepherd Jesus Christ (Acts 20:28; 1 Peter 5:2). As we've already discussed, shepherds were leaders entrusted to protect and feed their flock. Those called to shepherd are to protect God's people from false teachers and teachings and to feed them God's Word.

Can women be shepherds or have the gift of shepherding? Has Beth Moore shepherded the women in her church and around the world to whom she has taught God's Word? I believe so. Why? Because being a shepherd is not gender-specific. It is a metaphor that is descriptive of a person's role, which comes as a result of receiving the gift of shepherding. It doesn't matter whether or not the sheep are children, youth, adults, senior adults, men or women; they are still God's sheep. And those who shepherd them are their pastors.

TEACHERS

In Greek, the words translated "shepherds" and "teachers" are purposely joined together with a simple "and." While Paul makes a distinction between pastors and teachers, he joins them in such a way to show they are closely linked. Since God's people have access to God's Word and the Holy Spirit, why do they need teachers? If God's Word is made plain, are teachers even necessary? The Bible tells us yes! We've already mentioned Huldah in this chapter, but it is worth doing so again. Even though the king heard the Law read and God convicted him through his Word, he still sent for someone to explain it to him. Priscilla and Aquila took Apollos aside to teach him more adequately about the gospel. And what about Philip and the Ethiopian eunuch in Acts 8? Even though the eunuch is reading Isaiah, he asks Philip to explain it to him so he can understand. In this example, we see the interplay between the gifts of evangelism and teaching.

In 1 Corinthians 12:28, Paul lists teachers as third in importance: apostles, prophets, then teachers. Teachers are those who are able to teach Christ by teaching God's Word and the basic Christian teachings of the church. Thielman writes, "In Ephesians, to sit under this teaching is simply to 'learn Christ,' a phrase that probably refers to learning the basics of the gospel about Christ as well as its ethical implications."[8] Perhaps more so now than ever, we need teachers of God's Word because we are separated from the world of Scripture by language, culture, time, place, and people. The context of Scripture is completely foreign to modern-day Western societies. We also live in a postmodern, post-Christendom world. Before we can teach what something means today, we must first seek to understand what it meant then.

One of the problems today is that many people think all you need to be a teacher is a Bible. The blogosphere turns every woman who desires to be a teacher of Scripture into one. The one who has authority to teach is the one with the most charisma, the biggest following, the largest platform, and the highest number of hits. Everyone wants to be a teacher! Rather, we should take seriously the warning in James 3:1: "Not many of you should become teachers, my fellow believers, because you know that we who teach will be judged more strictly." As Hebrews 10:31 reminds us, "It is a dreadful thing to fall into the hands of the living God." Church historian Timothy George says, in regard to this verse and the calling to teach and preach God's Word, "To be a minister of the gospel in the service of such a calling, such a word, is high and holy, but it's also scary and dangerous and fraught with all kinds of problems . . . [This calling] should not be undertaken lightly or unadvisedly but . . . entered into advisedly, carefully, prayerfully, and in the fear of God."[9]

The New Testament has much to say about false teachers. False teaching destroys God's church. Consider the following analogy. A few years ago, I was diagnosed with ulcerative colitis, which means that parts of my colon have tears that cause me to bleed. Certain foods can make my disease worse, especially too many things that would cause constipation, but also some foods that help with constipation! If I ate a diet of only breads, sugar, high fiber, and fatty foods, my disease would probably worsen. A diet of only these foods over time could even lead to serious complications or death.

False teaching is spiritual food that kills. If God is truth, then anything false is godless. It does not come from the only true God: Father, Son, and Holy Spirit. The church does not necessarily need more teachers; she needs more teachers called by God, gifted by God, and trained to teach the truth of God. What the church needs none of are false teachers. I become so sad and angry when I hear and see men and women give false teaching to God's sheep, for they are killing the very people for whom God the Son died. Those gifted and called by God to teach need to be adequately trained (chapter 5, humble learners). We will discuss this more in the next chapter, so hang tight.

We've come to the end of the list of those God calls to his service in Ephesians 4. Additional spiritual gifts exist, and you can explore these if you choose to do so via one of the suggested exercises below. But I believe if you are called to the kind of gospel ministry defined in this book, you will have at least one of these gifts, if not more.

However, before we conclude this look at the gifts, here is one last question we need to consider: *Where does preaching fit in all of this?* It obviously involves aspects of teaching and shepherding, but how does the task of preaching fit in with these various callings?

PREACHERS

Preaching is of central importance to the spreading of God's kingdom. Jonah was said to preach repentance (Jonah 3:1–5). John the Baptist went around preaching the kingdom of God. Jesus himself preached the kingdom of God: "'I must proclaim the good news of the kingdom of God to the other towns also, because that is why I was sent.' And he kept on preaching in the synagogues of Judea" (Luke 4:43–44). Paul's ministry was also one of preaching. Preaching is similar to the gift of evangelism in that the content of preaching must always involve the good news of Jesus Christ, who takes away our sins. Preaching is heralding a message that has been entrusted to you. Christian preaching is proclaiming the good news of Jesus Christ.[10] The New Testament does not seem to be as concerned with the *form* of preaching or how it is packaged, as it is about the *content* of preaching. Paul charges Timothy to "Preach the word" (2 Tim. 4:2). Preaching is a gift that I would add to this list of gifts given to those who have a formal ministry of the Word of God for the people of God.

But can women have the gift of preaching? Ann L. Bowman writes, "Nowhere does Scripture say that gifts are gender-based; rather, all are available to men and women alike. Sometimes confusion exists on this issue because gifts have been equated with church office, but these are not the same."[11] Spiritual gifts are not gender-based because the Spirit of God is not divided along gender lines. This is why we discussed at length the prophecy of Joel as it is retold in Acts. The Spirit comes down equally on men and women, and as a result, both men and women exhibit the same gift, namely prophecy.

For many years I was afraid to use the word *preaching* to describe my gift or how I exercised my call in part, because I equated preaching with being a senior pastor. My dad, who has been a senior pastor for most of my life, was more often called "Preacher" than he was "Pastor." While in seminary, I would tell people who asked about my calling that I felt gifted in writing and *speaking*. But I came to realize that the opportunities I was given to "speak" on God's Word, opening up the text and expounding on it, was in fact preaching. In a sense, whatever we call it does not much matter ("A rose by any other name would smell as sweet."[12]). More important is the actual act, whether it fits with what the Bible describes as preaching. The preaching gift doesn't metamorphose into speaking when a female exercises the gift instead of a man, or when the audience changes from men to women or from adults to youth. Preaching, like these other gifts, is given to both men and women.

THE PURPOSE OF THE GIFTS

The differences between each gift are subtle. They are all shades of the same color: to communicate and proclaim God's Word. They are descriptive of a ministry of the Word.[13] What, then, is the goal or purpose of these spiritual gifts? Christ has put in place people with these gifts to equip the saints for works of service or "the work of ministry" (Eph. 4:12), as the ESV translates it. The goal of these gifts is to assist God's people in their own callings and ministries for the building up and unity of Christ's body until the work is completed when Christ returns.

The primary reason God calls and gifts us for this type of ministry is for the equipping of God's people, in turn, for ministry. All of God's people are called to ministry. When God calls us into relationship with himself, he also calls us to serve as ministers in every aspect of life. Theologian Karl Barth says, "Rather, the whole church, the community of all the saints together, is the clergy appointed by God for a ministry to and for the world."[14]

Even though the calling we are addressing in this book is a call to serve as a spiritual leader speaking God's Word authoritatively for the people of God, it does not mean we are ministers and the rest of God's people are not. Perhaps you grew up in a church where the leadership made this distinction: those on the church staff "did" ministry, and the rest of the church were recipients of that ministry. However, this is not what we find in Scripture. Rather, all God's people are called to minister and proclaim the holy and true gospel of Jesus Christ to others.

All of God's people are therefore given gifts to use for the ministry of the church and its mission in the world. The distinction is that the gifts mentioned in verse 11 are called to help *prepare* God's people to faithfully minister. As preachers, teachers, and evangelists, we prepare the people of God to become evangelists in their workplaces, teachers at home, and preachers to friends and neighbors. The work of ministry is for all members of the church of God, the bride of Christ. Those who *shepherd* God's people with a ministry of the Word do so, so that together they may build up the body of Christ.[15]

When your calling is rooted in the mission of God as it is revealed in Christ, then it frees you up from making your calling all about you. It frees you from feeling like you need to be on a pedestal or at a higher level than others. Instead, it places you on the floor next to Jesus with a bowl of water and a towel, washing the feet of others. A call to minister to ministers is a call of service to the glory of Jesus Christ.

HOW CAN YOU DISCOVER YOUR SPIRITUAL GIFTS?

So now for the question you probably have been waiting to ask: *How do I know if I am gifted, and for what?* If you are looking for an easy answer like "Do steps 1, 2, and 3," then you might be disappointed. Remember, we cannot manufacture or manipulate our callings nor put God into a box and work out his gifting like an algebra formula. At the same time, determining spiritual gifts is a topic competently covered in other literature, and I highly encourage you to read some more on this topic from others who are more knowledgeable on the topic.[16] But before you get discouraged that your question has gone unanswered, I want to highlight the context in which you will be able to discern your spiritual gifts.

Paul tells a young Timothy, "Do not neglect your gift, which was given you through prophecy when the body of elders laid their hands on you" (1 Tim. 4:14). Our gifts will be discovered only within the community of the church. Some denominations, like mine, will put together discernment committees for those who feel called to ministry. If your church or denomination does not do this, then you need to engage people in the church who will surround you, pray for you, and acknowledge the gifts they see. These gifts will become evident to you and to them as you become involved in the ministry of the local church. (We will discuss this in more depth in chapter 8.)

My friend Leslie Ann Jones, whom I mentioned in chapter 1, shares this story about how one of her seminary professors helped her see the gifts God had given her:

> Robert Smith, Jr. also had a profound effect on my sense of calling. He's hands-down one of the best preachers in the world, and because I knew that, I was terrified to take his preaching class. I'm an introvert who would rather sit behind a computer and write words than stand in front of people and speak them. But Dr. Smith called something out of me that I didn't know was there. He looked at me and named my gifts and showed me how to use them. The fact that he, a master preacher and true man of God, believed in me and saw the Lord's hand on me helped me to believe that my calling was real. Even now, nearly ten years later, Dr. Smith's confidence, not in me but in God's work in me, pushes me to trust in God's faithfulness to enable those he has called to the ministry. Even me.[17]

Spiritual gifts tests can be helpful, but at the same time should be used cautiously to help discern the gifting of the Spirit. There's a tendency to want to make spiritual gifts very distinct from one another with no overlap. Paul was an apostle, prophet, evangelist, preacher, pastor, and teacher (2 Tim. 1:11). Timothy was an evangelist, church planter, preacher, and teacher. We should not be overly stressed about determining which *one* gift we possess. Rather, if God is calling you to serve on his behalf for the people of God, delivering the Word of God, then he will most likely gift you with several of these gifts, like shepherding, prophesying, teaching, preaching, and evangelizing. Know this: the God who is calling you will gift you for the call he has given you. He will see it through.

WHAT DOES IT MEAN FOR US?

Just as I began, I want to reiterate that everyone we have studied so far in this book has a ministry of the word of God. The people God puts in charge of his church today also have a ministry of the Word. Although there are slight differences between prophets, evangelists, shepherds, teachers, and preachers, they are all given a ministry of the Word of God to equip God's people for ministry. I love what Karl Barth says: "Where there is no word of salvation, encouragement, direction, judgment—in short, without proclamation of the Messianic peace—there is no community of saints and no mission." [18] God is at work preparing his bride by raising up individuals to help him with this task.

Today our churches have made it so that we look at calling differently depending on our gender. Only senior pastors are shepherds, some may say. When a young man expresses a call to pastoral ministry, the path is laid out for him even if he never serves as a senior pastor (many young men serve in associate pastoral roles such as a youth minister or family minister). In a way, a call to ministry is simpler for men. But when it comes to women, many church leaders simply do not know what to tell women who sense a call to ministry. It is as if a big question mark is placed over them. Perhaps some church leaders would not hire a woman to fill a position that is a ministry of the Word, so they do not know what to say or how to encourage women in a call to ministry. In these cases, leaders might encourage women to pursue a call by volunteering in the church or pursuing a degree like education, psychology, or counseling. Perhaps this has been your experience.

As I have said before, God calls us and equips us with gifts needed for the call. Despite what the church communicates verbally and nonverbally, you do not have to be a senior pastor to preach or teach. Likewise, you do not have to be a senior pastor to shepherd. Women need shepherds. Youth need shepherds. Children need shepherds. Families need shepherds. The dying need shepherds. The sick need shepherds. The orphans need shepherds. The broken, abused, lost, and forgotten need shepherds. The immigrants need shepherds. The disabled need shepherds. Every person in the church needs shepherds. Unless it is a small church, the senior pastor of a church cannot adequately shepherd every person in his flock. So he or the supervising board hires shepherds to help him shepherd the people. I continue to pray that increasingly more churches will hire women who are called by God to help shepherd the flock. Many churches already do, so be encouraged.

If you have the gift of preaching and cannot preach on a Sunday behind a pulpit, that's okay. Perhaps God is calling you to preach to women. Perhaps God is calling you to preach to prisoners. Perhaps God is calling you to preach the gospel at a college or university. Preach the Word. Teach the Word. Evangelize the lost. Proclaim the good news of Jesus Christ, the kingdom of God, repentance, and the forgiveness of sins!

Lord Jesus Christ, assist us by your grace to be stead-fast, immovable, always abounding in your work, that we may be assured that in you our labor is never in vain. (Adapted from 1 Cor. 15:58 NKJV)

REFLECTION QUESTIONS

1. If spiritual gifts are not gender-based but given freely and equally to both men and women, how does this shed light on your understanding of what it means to be called to ministry?

2. Sometimes we might be tempted to use spiritual gifts to promote ourselves or to give us a bigger platform. What's the purpose of spiritual gifts? Where might you be tempted?

3. What connection do you see between our definition of calling and the spiritual gifts given to leaders of the people of God? Anything new or surprising?

DISCUSSION QUESTIONS

1. What spiritual gifts do you see in me? Why?

2. Have you struggled with matching a role or position to your gifts? How do you compensate in a job that might require a gift you do not have?

3. Do you think God still gives the gift of prophecy today? Discuss this part of the chapter.

PERSONAL EXERCISES

1. Read Romans 12:6–8, 1 Peter 4:10–11, or 1 Corinthians 12:1–31. What are some other spiritual gifts we didn't discuss? What observations can you make? Go deeper by studying these verses with the help of commentaries.

2. Ask your parents, others in your church, and your pastors what gifts they see in you. Is there a common theme? Talk to your pastor or youth pastor about ways you can use your spiritual gift(s) within the church.

3. Write down the names of some women (women you know personally or women you know through their ministries) who exhibit the different gifts mentioned in Ephesians 4:11–13. I already mentioned Anne Graham Lotz and Beth Moore. Who else could you add? Consider doing this exercise with your mentor.

MINISTRY SPOTLIGHT:

SHARON HODDE MILLER

Sharon Hodde Miller discerned her call to ministry while she was in college. During her freshman year, she became involved in a campus ministry and rose to leadership quickly. God used the combination of increasing opportunities, confirmation of her gifts, and overall passion for ministry to make her call clear. Her family was very supportive and affirming of her gifts, especially her father and mother.

During her first year out of college, Sharon worked for Proverbs 31 Ministries, a nonprofit Christian ministry for women. During that time, she learned a lot about women's ministry, especially by watching the president of Proverbs 31, Lysa TerKeurst, exercise her gifts. However, by the end of that year, Sharon realized her calling was taking her in a different direction. She loved to learn theology and the biblical languages, Greek and Hebrew. Sharon felt called to make those things accessible to women. So she decided to go back to school.

In the following years, Sharon earned her MDiv at Duke Divinity School, and then her doctorate of philosophy (PhD) at Trinity Evangelical Divinity School in Deerfield, Illinois. While at Trinity, Sharon did her PhD dissertation on the factors that influence women to pursue an MDiv at evangelical seminaries. She chose this topic out of a desire to cultivate the gifts of women in the church, and she discovered that many of the factors that affirmed her calling were also present in the lives of other women, like supportive relationships and hands-on ministry experience.

Today, Sharon is married to Ike, a pastor, and they have three children. She is also a writer and speaker. Sharon's first book, *Free of Me*, which is on the topic of self-forgetfulness, was published by Baker Publishing in 2017. She plans to write a follow-up book, and hopes to one day write a book on her doctoral research. In between writing books and raising her children, she blogs at SheWorships. com and writes for Christian outlets such as *Christianity Today*, Propel Women, and She Reads Truth, to name a few.

"Big picture, I want to help raise the bar of teaching for Christian women. I desire to draw women into a deeper faith, to chew on the meat of Scripture, and to live a message that is about so much more than ourselves," Sharon said.

When I asked her if she had any advice to share with you, Sharon said, "If you feel called, go. Many women experience fear, doubt, confusion, and guilt when they consider going into ministry, but this is completely normal. Not only are there plenty of examples of people in Scripture who were called by God and were also unsure about the call, but the majority of women wrestle with this too. Instead of listening to those fears, listen to the Holy Spirit, and listen to the feedback you receive from pastors, leaders, parents, and friends. If they see a calling in you, take them seriously. This is one of the primary ways God calls us: through his church."

CHAPTER 7

Do I Need a Theological Education?

Ten years ago I sat in a room at my church while a woman spoke to the girls in the youth group. I was in seminary at the time. Although she meant well, this woman had gone online and looked up definitions of English words in several Old Testament verses for her talk. Then, she used a Hebrew lexicon to find the original words in Hebrew. From there, she looked at the many definitions of those two words and chose the definitions that fit with what she wanted to say. The definitions she chose had nothing to do with the definition of those words in their context. She was making Scripture say what she wanted it to say, not what it really meant, by incorrectly using Hebrew words. She had changed the meaning of the text!

The problem we face today is that with the Bible in one hand and a computer and the internet in the other hand, we all think we have what is necessary to become an authoritative teacher of Scripture. You may have noticed this trend and perhaps have even thought, *Why do I need seminary?* Or, after reading the previous chapter, maybe you think theological training isn't necessary since God gives us spiritual gifts and his Holy Spirit.

Shortly after making my calling public to my local church at age fifteen, I told my parents I wanted to eventually go to seminary. That's what my father, a pastor, did after college. He went to seminary, and I wanted to follow in his footsteps. But once in college, I wasn't as zealous for seminary anymore. I didn't think I could "do" seminary; I wasn't sure I was smart enough. I was timid. By my junior year, I was a Christian studies major, and I thought what I was learning was sufficient training for ministry. But then my perspective changed. What convinced me to go to seminary?

IS THEOLOGICAL EDUCATION BIBLICAL?

You may be reading this chapter as an eleventh grade student thinking, *I'm just trying to make it through chemistry class, let alone high school, and I'm only now beginning to think about college. Seminary is too far away to consider right now.* If that's you, I get it. This chapter may be one you don't read all the way through now, but pick up later when you are ready to think about these things. I want this chapter to be a resource for you when you are faced with the question of what to do after college. I do not want you to be burdened now to have it all figured out.

For those of you who are ready to think about training after college, I want to convince you that the cost is worth it, that theological education is worth it, but even more importantly, that it is biblical. As I was praying and thinking through whether I should go to seminary, my Bible reading led me to 2 Timothy 3:14–16:

> But as for you, *continue in what you have learned* and have become convinced of, because you know those from whom you learned it, and how from infancy you have known the Holy Scriptures, which are able to make you wise for salvation through faith in Christ Jesus. All Scripture is God-breathed and is useful for teaching, rebuking, correcting and training in righteousness. (Emphasis mine)

Continue in what you have learned. I couldn't get past this command. As we have seen already, learning is necessary and a prerequisite for those who will be teachers and communicators of God's Word. It is also a lifestyle and an attitude that all of God's children should adopt.

A valid application of 1 Timothy 2:11–15 for women who feel called by God to have a teaching, shepherding ministry is a formal theological education. Paul urged the women in Ephesus to be humble learners of the apostolic teaching before teaching other women. How much more should those of us who are called to care for and feed God's sheep commit to learning as much as possible?

Meredith Teasley spent her first two years of seminary afraid to take biblical Hebrew and preaching classes, but retrospectively she is thankful for the training and relationships the program provided. After graduating with her MDiv, Meredith moved to Virginia to serve in a church plant as the children's minister. Just one year later, her dream job became a reality—to serve at LifeWay as a full-time camp specialist. "Camp ministry and children's ministry may not seem like the best places to use my academic studies, but my education was critical," Meredith said. "I'm grateful for the theological training to equip leaders, to work with many different kinds of churches, and even to communicate deep, theological truths in a kid-friendly way without watering down the gospel story."[1]

None of the people we studied in Scripture were required to go to seminary, you might say, so why should we? First, people in Scripture did receive theological education but of a different kind. They received direct speech and visions from God. Moses' theological education took place on a mountain. Mary's took place in her home. Paul's took place on a road and afterwards.

MINISTRY IS SERIOUS BUSINESS

Theological training is necessary to prepare you for the responsibility of your call. As a minister of the gospel of Jesus Christ, you will be charged with the *caring of souls*. Let that sink in. You will bear the responsibility of speaking on behalf of God by expounding God's Word, and you will bear the responsibility of shepherding and protecting God's sheep from wolves. James's warning should reverberate in our ears and cause us to proceed cautiously. Those of us who are called to shepherd, teach, protect, and watch over God's sheep will be held to a higher standard than the sheep themselves. We will be judged more strictly. We should feel the weight of our callings so that we take them seriously. Soul care is serious business. Like physicians, especially surgeons, who feel the life-and-death weight of their callings, we, too, should feel the *eternal* life-and-death weight of our callings, just as much and possibly more. Like a mother who entrusts her baby to a caretaker, God is entrusting the very people he created and died for to us, to care for until he returns.

My friend Hayden Walker has served as youth minister at a Baptist church in Birmingham for several years. She wrote to me, "Ministry is hard work, and it should be more than just event planning. My theological education reminds me that I have a responsibility to the gospel and to communicate truth, not just coordinate a calendar."[2]

Given this responsibility, we want to be prepared for the calling at hand. We need seminary training because the Bible will never mean something today that it didn't mean in its original context. We are separated from the world of the Bible by thousands of years and by place, culture, language, religion, and more. We need the right tools to help us faithfully interpret Scripture. We do not want to misrepresent God or his Word, and we definitely do not want to feed God's sheep false teaching. Seminary teaches us the languages, culture, and background of Scripture. It also teaches us genre and how to read Scripture, and how to see the Bible as one theological composition. It teaches us church history, the creeds and about orthodoxy, the beliefs that one must hold to be a Christian.

Going back to 2 Timothy 3:14–16, as ministers of the gospel we are called to study, learn, and grow in knowledge of the Bible. How will we ever be able to teach the Bible if we are not first students of the Bible? If we do not engage in serious study of Scripture from orthodox, biblical scholars, we can be more susceptible to teaching what we want the Bible to say or simply "what it means to me" without the support of scholarship or church history. How will you teach Proverbs and Ecclesiastes? Are you prepared to teach the Law of Moses or Revelation? Your teaching will be limited by the knowledge you do and do not have. So, just like Paul tells Timothy, continue in what you have learned. A serious calling requires serious study of Scripture.

SEMINARY TRAINING AS A GIFT AND AN OFFERING

Seminary is both a gift from God and an offering to God. As someone who loves God's Word, once I was in seminary I began to see that the opportunity to study God's Word exclusively and deeply from Bible scholars was a gift! I felt like Mary sitting at the feet of Jesus through the opening up of Scripture. In some respects, I never wanted my time in seminary to end. I could not get enough of learning God's Word. I wanted more and more.

Once I viewed seminary as a gift, I also saw it as an opportunity to give back to God, for God and his vocation deserved my best. If doctors are required to go to medical school, if lawyers are required to go to law school, if certified counselors are required to go to graduate school, then why should I, someone called to ministry, not go to divinity, or ministry, school? If these professionals require the very best training, then so should ministers of the church who will speak about the Living God and deliver his Word to others. To give three years of my life to careful preparation and study was my way of saying to God that I thought my calling was worth the sacrifice.

Although I was a Christian studies major as an undergraduate, I knew God had not received my very best in college. I was overly involved with campus ministry, my social club, volunteer work, and other coursework. I needed to mature; I needed to go further up and further in. God's calling was a high calling, and it deserved the best preparation.

WHAT YOU LEARN HAS ETERNAL VALUE

Theological education is necessary for those who are called to gospel ministry because it has eternal value. When you look at the value of theological education from a worldly perspective, the payout may not justify the cost. But when you view training from a heavenly perspective, giving three years of your life to God and the study of his Word is worth it. Jesus lived thirty years before having a public ministry that lasted only three years. Studying God's Word, theology, and ministry within a community of believers is never a waste; it's always worth the time and expense.

Paul begins his first letter to the Corinthians by telling them the gospel is foolishness to the world but wisdom to those being saved. Paul writes, "Has not God made foolish the wisdom of the world? . . . For the foolishness of God is wiser than human wisdom, and the weakness of God is stronger than human strength" (1 Cor. 1:20, 25).

If this is true of the gospel, then it is right to expect that being a minister *of* the gospel will also be viewed as foolish to the world. Ministry training will be foolish to the world. Giving your life to a ministry of the gospel will be foolish to the word. But if you believe the gospel isn't foolishness but the wisdom of God, then giving three years of your life to the study of the wisdom of God is worth it. You can't put a price tag on theological training; it is priceless. It will never be a waste.

OBSTACLES TO THEOLOGICAL TRAINING

At least three American cultural ideals have made their way into the Christian church: *Have it now. Have it easy. Have it all.* We want things to happen fast. Therefore, we have fast food, microwaves, fast downloading capabilities, and fast cars. We do not want to wait for anything good. We want it now.

We also do not want to work hard for things. We want to lose weight easily. We want to get ahead easily. We want things handed to us.

We want it all. We want what our parents have at their ripe age of fifty or sixty by the time we reach thirty. We want it all—the perfect house with a high-paying job and vacations that take us around the world. It's difficult to separate these three strands because they wrap around one another like the threads of a rope. We want to have it all now and easily.

What does this have to do with a call to ministry? We may choose a seminary based on convenience and not on conviction. We may be tempted to choose a ministry job based on the salary package rather than where God wants us.

However, we have seen through our survey of Scripture that a call to ministry is never fast, easy, or everything a person desires it to be. Abraham is promised a land he never gets to inherit; he is promised a nation he never gets to see. Moses is never able to bring the people into the promised land. David has to wait approximately fifteen years from his anointing as king to the day he takes the throne, and then he never gets to see the building of the temple. The worldview of Scripture clashes with our own, and what often results is an internal storm. We are pulled by our culture even as we are pulled by our knowledge and commitment to Scripture and God.

These three strands—have it now, have it easy, have it all—can also affect how we view our callings. We may want our callings to come about quickly and easily and to be everything we want them to be. It may be easy to rationalize skipping out on seminary by choosing to see it as a waste of time or money, or as an obstacle to fulfilling your call *now*. Seminary is neither easy nor fast. It's designed to mirror ministry and teach you what it will be like: hard and slow.

I remember calling my dad the week before my third semester finals in seminary. I complained that I was overwhelmed by all the papers and tests while also working a part-time job. It was *too* hard, and I wanted to give up. My dad, having been in ministry for more than two decades, perceptively told me, "Kristen, God is using these experiences to teach you now what it means to depend on God and to not give up in the hard times so that when you experience the difficult times in ministry later, you will remember that the power of God that has carried you now will carry you through in the future." He was right. As I have faced challenges in my ministry journey since graduating from seminary, I am grateful that I had a hard, slow theological training experience, because it has prepared me for the difficult, slow journey of ministry.

SHOULD WOMEN GO TO SEMINARY?

Before we move into the practical portion of this chapter, let's consider one last question that some of you may be asking: *Can I go to seminary as a* woman? By now the answer may be obvious (yes!), but my sense is that for some of you, this question is still an obstacle. So let's recap what we have concluded thus far in this book about women and a call to gospel ministry.

First, God called women to leadership ministries in Scripture, which increased in number from the Old Testament to the New Testament. Second, in the age of the Holy Spirit, God's Spirit calls and leads both men and women into Word-based ministry. Third, spiritual gifts aren't gender-based. Fourth, Scripture doesn't teach that higher learning is reserved for only men. Christianity is not a caste system! God's Word and revelation of himself is for all. Fifth, in keeping with the spirit of 2 Timothy 3:14–16 and the rest of Scripture, all who handle God's Word must learn how to handle it properly.

When I was considering whether or not I should even go to seminary, I was convinced I had greater chances of being taken seriously as a woman in ministry if I had theological education. Like young Timothy, to whom Paul said, "Don't let anyone look down on you because you are young" (1 Tim. 4:12), I didn't want anyone to look down on me because I was a woman. I had personally witnessed the lack of theological education and depth among female teachers, and I wanted to be a theologically trusted co-worker in ministry. Besides, women and children in the church deserve—just as much as men—to have teachers of Scripture who are theologically trained. And if male ministers are required to have seminary training, so should female ministers.

SEMINARY OR DIVINITY SCHOOL?

But what exactly is theological education?, you may be asking. Theological education usually refers to graduate-level education focused on training men and women for gospel ministry in the church. Theological education includes courses in the Bible, theology, biblical languages, church history, preaching, pastoral counseling, missions and evangelism, and the like. Theological education takes place in a seminary or divinity school. Often, though not always, a seminary is a school that is tied to a particular denomination and that readies candidates for ordination. For example, the Southern Baptist Convention has six seminaries. Presbyterians, Anglicans, Methodists, and other denominations all have their own seminaries. Some exceptions, such as Gordon-Conwell Theological Seminary, are not connected to only one denomination.

Divinity schools, on the other hand, are usually interdenominational or multi-denominational. This means that students come from a variety of denominations. Divinity schools are also connected to a university. My alma mater, Beeson Divinity School, is on the campus of Samford University. Trinity Evangelical Divinity School is on the campus of Trinity International University. Duke Divinity School is on the campus of Duke University, and so on.

However, the way we use the word *seminary* is equivalent to the way those of us in the southern United States use the word *Coke*. I call all carbonated sodas "coke," even though it is the name for one particular soda, Coca-Cola. Seminary is often used colloquially to refer to any graduate-level theological school that prepares ministers of the church.

ONLINE OR ON CAMPUS?

Before we discuss how to choose a seminary and what questions to ask, I want to encourage you to do your education in person and not online, if possible. Almost every institution now offers degrees online. Online degrees are useful if you are in a place or situation where it is your only option for training. Perhaps you are married and your husband has an established career in a place that does not have a theological institution. Your only option to learn theology and Scripture is online. This is the true purpose of online degrees—to make seminary possible for those who otherwise would not be able to receive theological training. However, some students choose online programs because they are convenient; you never have to leave your pajamas or couch if you don't want to. But ministry is not convenient! We are not called to convenience but to sacrifice.

The ideal situation is to receive a theological education in person. If ministry happens person-to-person, face-to-face, and heart-to-heart, so should your training for ministry. Something transformative happens in the classroom, where you can see facial expressions, engage with the professor, and talk to students after class. Theological education at its best is done in community. Paul House is helpful in explaining this:

> The Bible highlights face-to-face theological education. God sent his son, not just his Word. Moses, Elijah, Huldah, Jesus, Barnabas, Paul, Aquila, and Priscilla mentored future servants of God. They did so face-to-face in community settings. They did so individually and in groups. They ate together. They prayed and worshipped God together. They suffered and shared together. They did use the medium of writing to advance their mission, but always to supplement synchronous education conducted in the same location as the learners. Jesus was able to send twelve disciples and then seventy disciples through such personal means. The early church multiplied disciples and ministers in this fashion.[3]

My apartment burned down during the week of finals my first semester at Beeson. Our Student Government Association had already planned a Christmas party the following weekend. Unbeknownst to me, the students collected gift cards and money and put them on a little Christmas tree. They gave it to me at the party. Because I did my education in person, my seminary community was able to minister to me in person at a time of crisis. This experience taught me how to minister to others.

Attending seminary in person is challenging, especially for those who are married and have children. Attending seminary remotely is better than not attending seminary at all. But if it's simply a matter of convenience, let me ask you this: Are you willing to move across the country or across the world to serve Christ in ministry wherever he places you? If yes, then I hope you will consider moving to the seminary to which God is calling you when that time comes. It will be an opportunity to practice obedience and trust so that when God calls you to a place even further away, it will be easier to take that next step.

HOW DO YOU CHOOSE A SEMINARY?

Where does one begin in choosing a seminary from among all the wonderful options? I want to provide some questions I think are important to ask when looking at different seminaries.

The first question to ask is, do I want to stay in a seminary within my own denomination or one that is inter-or multi-denominational? Another way to phrase this question is, who do I want to shape me? The positives of going to a seminary within your denomination is that you will be shaped by the top thinkers within your denomination. For example, if you are Anglican, you will perhaps become even more firmly Anglican. If you are Presbyterian, you will perhaps leave seminary even more Presbyterian. In addition, if you want to be ordained, a denominational seminary will (usually) get you there faster, and some denominations who ordain women will not ordain you unless you go to one of their seminaries.

On the other hand, most evangelical interdenominational seminaries want their students to leave as they entered: as good members of their respective denominations. But these institutions believe that there is value in being shaped by Christians of other denominations. They say, "We want to teach you how to be a good

Baptist while learning to be ecumenical." Ecumenism is the promotion of unity across denominations. As one of my professors used to say in class, "We are all different regiments in the same army!"

What Is the MDiv Degree?

After deciding the type of school you are interested in attending, you'll want to look at the types of degree programs the school offers. Ask yourself, which program should I choose? The most appropriate degree for most types of pastoral ministry is the MDiv, or master of divinity. This has been the case for much of the history of theological education in North America.

What courses will you take for an MDiv degree? Although this will depend partly on the individual school, most evangelical institutions will offer biblical languages, church history, systematic theology, preaching, and pastoral care.

If you will be teaching God's Word through the mediums of writing, speaking, preaching, or teaching, the MDiv will provide a better grasp of the biblical languages. Two or three classes in Greek or Hebrew is not enough. You won't retain it nor know how to use it when you are preparing to teach Scripture. You need not only to learn the languages but know *how* to use them for preaching and teaching.

The MDiv degree will also require you to take preaching classes. If preaching is a spiritual gift you think you might have, you need the training and the practice. Even if you do not imagine yourself as a preacher, preaching classes will give you the tools to interpret, apply, and communicate Scripture. You can use these skills in many different areas of ministry and in conjunction with many other gifts. The MDiv degree as a whole is designed to be comprehensive and deep.

One of the benefits of a larger seminary is that if you are called to a very specific type of ministry, you can customize or specialize your MDiv degree. One of the benefits of a divinity school is that it usually offers joint degrees with the university. However, beware of institutions who have cheapened their MDiv degree, ones where you have to take only a couple of classes in both languages. Beware of a degree that is cheap, quick, and easy. Ask yourself, what am I losing? What will I miss out on? Is this degree the best I can get?

Consider the Faculty-to-Student Ratio

Next ask yourself, who are the faculty, and will I get to know them? Who will be the people who shape me? Read up on the faculty members at the various seminaries. What have they written? What do they teach or what is their specialization? But perhaps most importantly, will you get to know them on a personal level?

Large seminaries may have some of the best scholars in the field (a huge positive!), but one negative of a very large seminary is that you run the risk of not being able to know your professors on a personal level, and it may require more effort on your part to get to know the ones you do.

One of the benefits of attending a small seminary, for me, was not only sitting at the feet of biblical scholars in class but getting to know each one personally. When you are one of fourteen students in a class, you are able to ask more questions and be more involved with the teaching.

Some seminaries require students to meet weekly in a mentor group with a professor and other students. For a whole year, the mentor group can do life together: pray, eat, and talk about the Bible and life. Basically, they are doing incarnational, theological education. A school that offers students opportunities to be mentored by faculty outside the classroom is a positive worth considering.

While writing this book, I asked one of my former New Testament professors a question about Romans 16. He graciously sent me a section of the commentary on Romans he had written for Zondervan that had yet to be published. The greatest value of seminary for me has been this: lifelong relationships with scholars who are invested in my life and ministry and continue to pray for me. You cannot put a price tag on that.

Financial Considerations

You'll also want to consider cost. You might be thinking to yourself that this is the first question to ask. But sometimes, if we know the cost up front, it can scare us away from truly examining a place. When you examine the cost, consider the following:

- The actual cost—not just tuition, but books, fees, housing, and more.
- Scholarships. Most schools offer a lot of scholarships. Also, many churches offer scholarships. Ask about scholarships given by churches near the school you are interested in. National scholarships are also available; consider these.
- Cost of living. What is the cost of living in the area where the school is located? Does the school offer housing, or will you have to find housing off campus? Often, larger seminaries will provide campus housing, which is a benefit to consider.
- Work. Will I have to work while in seminary? How much would I have to earn to make ends meet? Can I receive federal work-study?
- Loans. How many loans will I have to take out?
- Weigh the costs against the value. If you are comparing two schools that you think offer the same value of degree and theological formation, then cost may be the deciding factor. If you are comparing two schools that are not equal in value or in cost, you will need to decide which factor is most important to you.

Attitude Toward Women

You'll also want to consider the school's beliefs and attitudes about the role and place of women in gospel ministry. Do not expect to go to a seminary where every male student is supportive of you and of women in ministry, even if you do not feel called to be a senior pastor. You will (most likely) encounter opposition at some point. The ethos is more positive at some schools than at others. Consider these questions when examining seminaries: Are there any women on the faculty? What does the school say, if anything, about women? What do they believe about women in ministry as an institution? Talk to female students and alumnae from those schools. Ask the director of admissions how the school views its calling to prepare women for ministry. If its view concerning women is so limited that they say you are not called to ministry unless it's as a pastor's wife, or that your *only* ministry is in the home, then you will probably encounter more opposition and less encouragement. On the other hand, beware of those schools where you find a lot of women who are angry toward men. These schools probably have other red flags when it comes to preparing you for ministry.

Other Considerations

Consider additional factors when choosing a seminary. Who are the alumnae and how does the school help with job placement after graduation? Where is the school located? Are there ministries or churches in the area that would offer internships in areas of your interest? How does the school help guard and nurture you spiritually while you are a student? Does the school view theological education as information or formation or both? How does the school foster community?

There will be no perfect school, for we are imperfect people. You will find negatives and positives for both seminaries and divinity schools, large schools and small schools. But ask yourself, where can God get my best? Where can God best prepare me for the ministry to which he has called me?

PUTTING IT ALL TOGETHER

The summer before my senior year in college, I interned at First Baptist Church in San Antonio, Texas. During that summer, I had dinner with the pastor and his wife, and I mentioned I was considering seminary. The pastor encouraged me to pursue seminary and suggested one I had never heard of: Beeson Divinity School.

Later, back at college for my senior year, I made an appointment with the dean of the Christian Studies department. I asked him for a seminary recommendation. He, too, suggested Beeson Divinity School. A few weeks later, I traveled to North Arkansas to help lead a Discipleship Now weekend. The guest preacher for the weekend announced that he had come from none other than Beeson Divinity School.

How did I choose a seminary? I like to say that God chose the seminary and then told me his choice. He used three different people who did not know one another to recommend the school I would later attend.

As you consider seminaries, I encourage you to do the first exercise at the end of the chapter), pray, pray, pray. While I hope the criteria above is helpful, it should never be used apart from prayer. Seek the God who has called you into his service. Ask him to show you where you should be shaped for the ministry to which he has called you. Ask him to open doors and close doors. Ask him to raise red flags and to raise green flags. Ask him to speak through the mouths of mentors and other trusted people. Ask him to guide and to lead you, and trust that he will. For this is in keeping with the character of God. I like the ESV's translation of Psalm 138:8. May this verse encourage you and be your prayer:

> The LORD will fulfill his purpose for me; your stead-
> fast love, O LORD, endures forever. Do not forsake the
> work of your hands.

REFLECTION QUESTIONS

1. Have you ever considered seminary before? If not, why not? List any fears or excuses you may have for not attending seminary.

2. No one in the Bible had the kind of theological education we have today, but it doesn't mean they didn't have any theological training. What kind of training did those who were called to ministry receive?

3. What is the connection between the weight of our calls and being prepared for ministry?

DISCUSSION QUESTIONS

1. Why did you go to seminary?

2. Where did you go and what were the reasons that led you there?

3. How did seminary prepare you for your calling?

4. What advice would you give to me as I think about seminaries?

PERSONAL EXERCISES

1. Go to www.ats.edu/member-schools and look up the listing of accredited theological schools. You can search alphabetically or by geography, denomination,

or degree. If you are interested in a seminary in your denomination, make a list of those you see. If you are interested in a divinity school that is interdenominational, make a list of those that interest you. Perhaps you are unsure. In that case, make a list of both. For detailed information about a school, click on the name of the school. What's the faculty-student ratio? What are the school's beliefs? What degrees do they offer? Have you heard or read what other people are saying about these schools? Find reviews. Talk to mentors or people you trust for recommendations. You can use the questions above as a guide.

2. If you are in college now, then ideally, by your junior year you should request more information from the admissions offices of some of the schools of your choice and go for a campus visit or Preview Day. You will never really know how you feel about a place until you go for a visit. Do not go to school somewhere you haven't visited unless you are living overseas or are in a situation where that's not an option.

MINISTRY SPOTLIGHT:

RENEE PITTS

Renee Pitts grew up in church and "found the life of the church endlessly interesting and fulfilling." So it was no surprise that as a college student at Samford University, while trying to decide on her vocation, she found a deep level of satisfaction and enjoyment taking classes in Christian religion. Given her love of learning the Bible coupled with her ability to connect well with people and her concern for people who were hurting, especially because of injustices, Renee began to sense God leading her into ministry. Although she did not know what that would look like later, she expressed this sense of calling to the ministerial staff at her church and made that call public, as was the custom in her context.

"I was trepidacious in this decision, because no female had made a public declaration about ministry in my church until that point," Renee said. "As people came up to the front of the church to give me their words of encouragement and support, the associate pastor, a serious and distinguished gentleman, approached me, shook my hand firmly, looked me in the eye, and said, 'I have been expecting this.' It was incredibly affirming."

The spring of her senior year at Samford, Renee began visiting seminaries. She realized she needed to learn and grow before she could be called upon to lead in ministry in any significant way. "I knew that although my church experiences had been incredibly formative and had helped move me forward in my commitment to Christ, I still needed both knowledge and skills and the time to develop them both," she said. After much searching, Renee chose a seminary because of its simple gospel commitment.

Her first ministry job out of seminary was at a nonprofit with ten hours on the side as a campus minister at a local community college. She found the nonprofit work to be draining but the college ministry work life-giving and purposeful. From that point on, all of her vocational decisions were based on moving her deeper into the work of campus ministry.

At the time of the writing of this book, Renee serves full-time at Samford as one of four campus ministers. Her work is focused specifically on mobilizing undergraduate students for global missions. She also directs a scholarship program for students called into vocational global missions. She spends most of her time in one-on-one meetings with students, fostering a blend of mentoring, friendship, and discipleship. Renee also develops educational programming about global missions to complement what students are learning in the classroom.

Perhaps the most unique aspect of her ministry is that she shares an office and ministry context with her husband, Brian, who also is a campus minister at Samford. Brian and Renee met as students in seminary. Renee did not expect that they would work alongside each other, but their common passion for student discipleship and vocational space is a blessing.

When I asked her what she would say to you, Renee responded, "I would absolutely affirm the importance of theological education in preparing for ministry. There is no substitute for that time spent being taught and mentored. I believe theological education is a significant factor in both long-term ministry effectiveness and perseverance. I would also encourage young women not to be afraid to consider small church positions as a great way to learn and grow in ministry, and to be patient as the Lord provides opportunities to move into new ministry jobs. Most people do not start off where they eventually end up serving, but there is always valuable perspective to be gained in any ministry context. It is also vitally important for women in ministry to have relationships in their lives (friends, family, spouse) that provide safety and an opportunity for vulnerability, particularly in ministry contexts that do not naturally provide this."

CHAPTER 8

The Benefits of Mentors and Internships

O ne of the greatest joys in my call to ministry so far, especially as it relates to this book project, was the opportunity
to disciple two young women in their own call to ministry. Several
years after God gave me the idea for this book, my husband suggested I try out the material on some girls in my church's youth
group who felt called to ministry. I approached the youth minister,
who told me that within the last several months, four young women
had expressed a call to ministry. He asked if I would mentor them.

For one year I met with them. Then, after that first year, two
of the girls asked if the mentoring relationship could continue.
I watched as these two young ladies, in tenth and eleventh grade
respectively, grew in the confidence and knowledge of their callings.
They both felt called to ministry, but in the beginning they were
unsure what that meant. Because one loved children, she assumed
she was called to children's ministry. The other thought her call was
to the mission field. Yet as their mentor, I was able to peer into their
lives from outside. I was able to see the gifts God had given them and
that perhaps God had more in store than they could even imagine.
But like a brand-new baby horse who wobbles as she stands, unsure
of her legs, these two young ladies were a little unsure, somewhat
wobbly in their gifts and callings at first. By God's grace I was able
to guide, push, and encourage them. I was also bold enough to
speak truth into their lives, even if it meant saying no or discourag-
ing them from a certain path.

That was six years ago. These two women have grown and
matured in remarkable ways since then. By the time this book

is published, they will have graduated from college. They understand that their callings are primarily for God's people, feeding them God's Word. That may happen by ministering to children or to youth. It may take the shape of being a missionary overseas. It may be that they live out their callings as women's ministers. But the avenue or the position is not the calling. The Word of God is the calling. Today they both feel more confident and encouraged in their calling to teach Scripture, and I am very proud of them. They are women called by God, devoted to God, and obedient to God and his call.

In the previous chapter we discussed the importance of theological training. This training is primarily focused on learning the Bible, theology, and church history. In this chapter we will discuss the importance of mentorships and of cultivating spiritual gifts through practical training for ministry today. Mentorships and internships together combine the kind of practical training needed for ministry. Most seminaries require internships and mentorships as part of their degree program, but you do not have to wait until seminary to start these.

WHAT ARE MENTORSHIPS?

The idea of mentors is nothing new. Think back to the people we have studied so far in this book and to other people in Scripture. Can you think of any mentoring relationships in Scripture? Let me name a few: Moses and Joshua, Eli and Samuel, Jesus and the Twelve, and Paul and Timothy.

What is the value of mentorship? First, good mentors have wisdom. This assumes, then, that the one who is doing the mentoring is older than the one being mentored. In some situations, though, this is not necessarily the case, such as if someone is called to ministry later in life. The one mentoring may not be older but would have more years of experience in ministry than the one being mentored. Nevertheless, the expectation is that your mentor will pass on wisdom to you. Titus 2:3–5 says,

Likewise, teach the older women to be reverent in the way they live, not to be slanderers or addicted to much wine, but to teach what is good. Then they can urge the younger women to love their husbands and children, to be self-controlled and pure, to be busy at home, to be kind, and to be subject to their husbands, so that no one will malign the word of God.

Paul tells Titus to urge the older women to train the younger women. In what are they to train the younger women? In acts of godliness. Paul gets both practical and specific here: how to love husbands and children, to be self-controlled and pure, to work at home, to be kind, to be submissive. The older women are to teach doctrine (as I argued in chapter 5) and to impart their wisdom to the younger women for the sake of God's Word (v. 5).

Second, mentees are to learn from their mentors' teaching and example. Paul continually reminds Timothy to remember the things he has learned from Paul when they were on their missionary journeys. He writes in 2 Timothy 3, "You, however, know all about my *teaching*, my way of life, my purpose, faith, patience, love, endurance, persecutions, sufferings . . . But as for you, continue in what you have *learned* and have become convinced of, because you know those from whom you *learned* it" (10–11, 14, emphasis mine). This reference to continue in what you have learned most likely not only refers to Paul's mentoring of Timothy but also to the mentoring by Lois and Eunice (Timothy's grandmother and mother in 2 Tim. 1:5). Mentors are teachers of both doctrine and godliness. They open God's Word with us, and they invite us into their ministries and homes so that we can watch how they interact with and treat others. Most importantly, though, they point us to Jesus.

Third, mentors are people who speak into our lives, pray for us, walk spiritually with us, and do life with us. You need someone who will speak truth into your life even when it is difficult to do so. You need someone who is committed to pray for you, to listen to you, to impart wisdom, and to teach you. Good mentors are invested in their mentees. A mentor enters into a mentoring relationship precisely because they see God at work in the mentee and because they feel God has called them to the relationship.

Think again of the mentor relationships between Moses and Joshua, Eli and Samuel, Jesus and the twelve disciples, Paul and Timothy. Those who were mentored eventually were sent out on their own. Like parents who teach and impart wisdom to their children for years with the hope and expectation that the children will one day leave the nest, mentors have an end goal in mind. They, too, hope and expect you will in time be ready to go out into ministry. The mentors in the four pairs of men mentioned only stopped mentoring because of their deaths. Some mentoring relationships are for life, while others are only for a certain period. Whether a mentoring relationship is long or short, the end goal is your maturity and readiness.

Hopefully you already have a mentor, and you have found the discussion questions at the end of each chapter helpful as you meet with your mentor. If you do not have a mentor yet, don't be discouraged. Even after you are done reading this book, you can still bring these discussion questions to a future mentor. If you do not have a mentor, you may be wondering how to choose one.

How Do I Choose a Mentor?

I remember periods of my life when I did not have a mentor. I specifically wanted a woman in ministry, and those were hard to come by in small-town settings or even in new cities where I was still trying to find my way around. Facebook, blogs, and helpful church websites were still a thing of the future. Also, I felt awkward approaching a woman I didn't know. At times in your life, you may be without a mentor. This is okay. In those interim periods, perhaps read a biography of a woman who was in ministry. Let her mentor you through her life story, while you pray for God to provide you a face-to-face mentor. Remember, God is faithful, and he loves you.

> Which of you, if your son asks for bread, will give him a stone? Or
> if he asks for a fish, will give him a snake? If you, then, though you

are evil, know how to give good gifts to your children, how much more will your Father in heaven give good gifts to those who ask him. (Matt. 7:9–11)

As you pray for a mentor, here are some qualities to keep in mind. First, look for someone who has done or is doing gospel ministry, especially in an area close to your interest. Perhaps you feel called to youth ministry. If so, then pray for a mentor in that field, and search for one, if possible. Second, look for someone who is respected by others and is mature in the faith. Does this person have a good reputation? Third, look for someone who is theologically educated. I think this is important because if you have a mentor without theological education, then she might not be as likely to encourage you toward that end. At the same time, keep in mind that mentoring does not take the place of devoted, focused training of Scripture from the teaching of scholars. Last, look for someone who will speak truthfully into your life with love.

Often internships and mentorships go hand in hand. What do I mean? Many mentorships come from internships. If you are interning in youth ministry at a church, then most likely one of the youth ministers will mentor you. But just as internships end, mentorships within internships often end simultaneously. Therefore, you do not necessarily need to wait for internships to find mentors.

WHAT ARE INTERNSHIPS?

So why internships? First, internships provide practice for what is to come. If God has called you to ministry, why not start now? A call to ministry doesn't have to wait until you are twenty-five or thirty or until you have graduated from seminary. Timothy, Silas, Barnabas, and Titus escorted Paul on his missionary journeys, watching Paul, learning from Paul, and ministering alongside him and under his tutelage. When Paul was later imprisoned in Rome, these men served in Paul's place at different churches. Paul writes both Timothy and Titus letters reminding them of and urging them to do what they learned from Paul in their respective church ministries. Likewise, Joshua was Moses' aide, serving alongside him and learning from him so that when it was his turn to lead the people, he was well prepared.

The same can be said of the twelve disciples. They "interned" under Jesus. While Jesus was still with them, he sent them out on short mission trips. Read Luke 9:1–6, 10 and Luke 10:1–17. In the first passage, Jesus sends out the Twelve. In the second, he sends out seventy-two disciples. They are given opportunities to practice ministry while Jesus is still on earth so that when he leaves, they will be ready to continue the ministry of Jesus.

Although we won't find a one-to-one correlation between modern-day internships and these examples from Scripture, what we see from Scripture is value in learning from and practicing ministry with someone older. Therefore, spend your spring breaks and/or summers invested in a ministry internship. My two best spring breaks during college were spent doing beach evangelism at Panama City Beach in Florida. I also knew I needed to spend my summers doing something that would have value later in life; I needed an internship to give me experience. Each ministry internship opportunity allowed me to see where God had gifted me and to put those gifts into use.

Second, internships provide clarity to your call. Sometimes you can discern through an internship that maybe God isn't calling you to a specific area of ministry or to ministry at all. Other times God continues to affirm he is calling you to ministry or even to a specific area of ministry. One piece of clarity I received through my internships was about my love of teaching Scripture. I came to life when I had opportunities to teach. The audience didn't necessarily matter to me. Whether it was teaching VBS to preschoolers or a Bible study to college students, I felt satisfaction from teaching God's Word. Simultaneously, I realized I wasn't necessarily called to an age group, like children, youth, or college students. I was called to a ministry of God's Word.

Third, internships open doors to future ministry positions.

This point may seem trite, but let me explain why it is true. The more experience you have in ministry from a young age, the better. It shows your commitment to the church and gospel ministry. Internships provide references who can speak to future churches about your calling, character, and commitment. Let's imagine a church is looking to hire a youth minister. One candidate has seminary training but no practical experience. The other candidate has seminary training *and* two years' experience in youth ministry. Who is the church most likely to hire?

I think often of the disciples who both sat at the feet of Jesus as students and served alongside him, learning from him how to heal, cast out demons, preach, have table fellowship with sinners, and care for the outcast. A good internship provides both immediate and future value.

How Do I Choose an Internship?

Whether you are in high school, college, or beyond, you may wonder how to choose the right internship for you. What do you look for in an internship? The following are some helpful questions to ask the person overseeing the internship. First, what will I do? Will I actually be given ministry opportunities, or will I be running errands and making coffee? Do not assume that just because you will be interning in a church or parachurch ministry that you will be given opportunities to do ministry. Ask what roles you will have in your internship. It is important to make sure your expectations about the internship are in line with the expectations of the person overseeing the internship. A red flag for you is if the one overseeing the internship cannot articulate the purpose of the internship or the intern's role. This might be an indication that the minister hiring is looking for an assistant rather than providing an intern with an opportunity for growth and experience in ministry.

Second, how intentional will my ministry experience be? Will I have the opportunity to use and sharpen my spiritual gifts? These questions flow out of the first question. The goal of a proper internship, in addition to ministering to God's people, is to provide experience for an individual interested in a certain field. Internships are simultaneously a blessing for the church and for the one entering the internship. You want an internship that is intentional in cultivating you as a God-called minister. You do not want an internship that is left to chance. You want an internship that will allow you to use your gifts and will play to your strengths. If your gift is teaching, then you want an internship that will give you many opportunities to teach. If your gift is shepherding, then you want an internship that will allow you to shepherd. Look for internships where the supervisor is intentional about providing you with many ministry opportunities.

Third, who will mentor me? Usually the person who will mentor you is the one overseeing the internship. However, because most overseers are male, what will your relationship look like with the supervisor? Will he meet with you and other mentees weekly to discuss ministry-related questions and issues? Will he give you feedback about your teaching? You want to be careful about entering into an internship where no one will meet with you weekly to discuss what you are learning and experiencing in ministry.

Fourth, will I be paid? If not, how will I be supported? Sometimes the value an internship provides is worth the time you spend, even if you are not paid. But if you are seeking an unpaid internship, then you need to ask how you will be supported. Will the church provide housing or food? Does your home church have a scholarship for young people who are participating in an unpaid ministry internship? Will your parents be supporting you financially, or will you need to send out support letters? If you depend on summers to make money to help pay for college, or if you will have to borrow money to live on during an internship, then my advice is to find a paid internship, or work a part-time job and do a part-time internship. If you decide to raise support one summer for an internship, you may want to choose a paid internship another summer. You may be called to serve as a missionary or church planter one day where you will have to raise support. Raising support will be good practice. However, it is also a lot of work and could distract from the internship itself. Consider this and other possible disadvantages before committing to an internship.

Do not be afraid to look outside your hometown for an internship. Some of my best experiences took me out of my comfort zone, far away from home, to places where I knew no one.

Perhaps you are reading this book in the middle of your tenth grade year of high school. Internships and perhaps even mentorships are still a thing of the future. What can you do now? Talk with your youth minister and perhaps even your pastor. Ask if you can take on a leadership role in the youth ministry or the church at large. Consider leading a Bible study at your high school or taking on a leadership role in an established ministry, such as the Fellowship of Christian Athletes.

Pray. Ask God to show you where you are to go. Your call to ministry begins the moment God calls you. It may not fully mature or materialize until later, but you can take steps now that will help prepare you for future ministry. Avoid thinking of your call to ministry as something that will happen "one day." Instead, think of it as beginning now. What are you waiting for?

"Fan into flame the gift of God . . . Guard the good deposit entrusted to you . . . Do your best to present yourself to God as one approved, a worker who has no need to be ashamed, rightly handling the word of truth." (2 Tim. 1:6, 14; 2:15 ESV)

REFLECTION QUESTIONS

1. Can you find other examples of mentorships/internships in Scripture in addition to the ones we looked at? Write out observations about these relationships, the value of them, and their purpose.

2. If God has called and gifted us, then why do we need internships and mentorships? How do internships and mentorships fit with our biblical understanding of ministry?

3. How are internships or mentorships an act of giving God our best? What would you say to someone who asks you this question?

DISCUSSION QUESTIONS

1. What internship experience was most valuable to you and why?

2. What advice would you give me in finding an internship?

PERSONAL EXERCISES

1. Connect with others your age who are called to ministry. Perhaps begin a Facebook group to share internship and mentor possibilities.

2. Pray and ask God for a mentor and/or internship. Ask others for recommendations, and look outside your church or town.

MINISTRY SPOTLIGHT:

ASHLEY GORMAN

Ashley Gorman became a Christian when she was eighteen and in college. Early on she understood that being a Christian meant having a life of ministry and making disciples, no matter one's vocation. She never separated being in Christ from being in ministry.

As Ashley grew in her faith, though, God began to lead her down the path of vocational ministry. She learned about her spiritual gifts; became more aware of her talents, skills, and passions; prayed; sought God's Word; and listened to the counsel and affirmation from other believers in her community.

Ashley is very passionate about God's Word, and over time she learned that her gifts centered around communicating God's Word through teaching, writing, and speaking. She also realized she has a passion for women, for teaching them how to read Scripture, helping them learn how to grow with God and develop their skills, and equipping them for ministry.

After college, Ashley served on staff as the women's coordinator at the college ministry in which she came to Christ. For four years she served on two university campuses—North Carolina State and the University of North Carolina at Chapel Hill—leading Bible studies, assisting with leadership development, mentoring key leaders, and teaching at large group levels. After four years, Ashley took a break from vocational ministry and worked in a hair salon. But she couldn't shake her calling to communicate God's Word.

She began writing Bible study curriculum, but she realized that since she was writing about Scripture, she needed to be as accurate and well-informed as possible. Ashley took writing about the Bible very seriously, so she decided to attend Southeastern Baptist Theological Seminary in Wake Forest, North Carolina, where, at the time of writing, she is completing an MDiv. While in seminary, she took a job with Docent Group, writing custom curriculum for various churches across the nation. In this role, Ashley has written small group guides, Bible studies, and series that paralleled the pastor's sermons. She also has been part of a team of women who started the first academic group for women on her seminary's campus, the Society for Women in Scholarship. In 2012, Ashley coauthored her first book, *The Book of Matches*, with one of her seminary professors.

Over the years, Ashley has been very faithful to serve in the local church, teaching biblical literacy classes, writing curriculum and articles, and working on women's discipleship studies and strategies. "The calling I just described has definitely been a journey," she said. "In certain seasons, I would only really exercise one or two of [my gifts] at a time. God developed them in me over time. Many doubts and fears rose up—mostly because the types of gifting I had were found in very few women around me. God had to walk me through all of that step-by-step."

Ashley continues writing and hopes to publish more books for women. She would also like to oversee and give vision to women's spiritual development in the church. Ashley is also a wife and foster mother, which are additional spheres for ministry.

When I asked her what words of wisdom she would like to give to you, Ashley said, "Don't wish away the season you are in. The Lord is charting your course, and in his great goodness over your life, his plan is custom-made for everything you need. Instead of just seeing this season as the stepping-stone to the next season that you think will really make you happy (though sometimes, yes, he uses this season to prepare you for that one), view this season for what it is! Fully dive into it. Be present. Take it for all it's worth."

CONCLUSION

IS GOD CALLING YOU? IF YES, THEN GO!

One of my favorite books is *The Horse and His Boy*, the fifth volume in the Chronicles of Narnia series by C. S. Lewis. Near the end of the book, there is a moving scene where the boy, Shasta, is riding his horse down a road at night, feeling completely exasperated. At his weakest moment Shasta senses the presence of Someone walking next to him, but he cannot see who it is. After comprehending that this visitor is not a ghost, Shasta shares his sorrows, including being chased by many lions.

> "Don't you think it was bad luck to meet so many lions?" said Shasta.
> The Voice answered, "There was only one: But he was swift of foot."
> "How do you know?"
> "I was the lion."[1]

The lions Shasta thought were trying to kill him were actually one Lion who was protecting and leading him down the path to his true family. Like Shasta, sometimes we see life at surface level, while Scripture gives us a heavenly perspective. We, like Shasta, are going down a path. Calling and vocational ministry is a journey. But from the beginning of the journey to its end, God is with us.

NOW WHAT?

We've come to the end of the book. So now what? Where do we go from here?

First, go forth in prayer. Jesus' ministry was marked by prayer. He often withdrew by himself to pray (Luke 5:16). Jesus prays before miracles, such as the feeding of the five thousand (Matt. 14:19) and raising Lazarus from the dead (John 11:41–42). His greatest test—his betrayal and death on a cross—was bathed in prayer. Jesus prayed in the garden; he prayed on the cross. He very likely prayed every step of the way. Jesus also taught his disciples how to pray (Matt. 6:9–13) and later urged them to pray so that they would not fall into temptation (Matt. 26:41).

Prayer is not a suggestion, an add-on, or a recommendation. Prayer is a command from Jesus himself. It is also a right, a privilege, a blessing, and a necessity for a *Christian* ministry. Prayer brings us into the royal court of our triune God. Sisters, if you want to have a ministry that mirrors Jesus' ministry, then prayer must be an essential component. Our ministries and our faith won't survive without prayer. But even when we don't know how to pray or what to pray, he is faithful to help us when we ask.

Second, go forth in trust and obedience. Jesus teaches us that our Father is good and trustworthy. Everything I have said in this book boils down to the goodness and sovereignty of God over our calls and ministries. Trust him to see the call he has given you through to its completion. Obey him, even if obedience is difficult and you don't understand why. Depend on him, fully trusting in the truth that God loves you and wants to involve you in the work of ministry.

One day the King will return and set everything right. There will be no need for stewards of God's people "for the Lamb in the midst of the throne will be their shepherd, and he will guide them to springs of living water, and God will wipe away every tear from their eyes" (Rev. 7:17 ESV). Do you catch the irony in this statement?

Jesus, the Lamb, will be the shepherd. Lambs aren't shepherds; they are shepherded! Here, again, Jesus is flipping the world upside down. The sacrificial lamb will be the shepherd of all people. He is our redemption and our God.

In Revelation 19, John sees a vision of a wedding between the Lamb and his bride. Who is his bride? The redeemed people of God—men and women. Whereas God's story and our story began in a garden, it now ends with a wedding in a city. Men and women, once again, are serving side by side as worshippers (Rev. 7:9–14) and as priests ministering, this time to their husband, Jesus Christ, the Lamb of God. Men and women together become the bride submitting to their husband (Rev. 19:6–9).

Sisters, "'the harvest is plentiful but the workers are few'" (Matt. 9:37). Many people have yet to hear the good news of Jesus Christ, and many in the church have yet to be discipled! There's work to be done, and if God is tenderizing your heart, calling you to be his ambassador, serving on his behalf for his people, then go! Get prepared for the long journey ahead in such a way that you will last until the end. And remember that God is the author and finisher of your faith and ministry. He holds you. He is with you.

On the pulpit at my church is a plaque that reads, "Woe to me if I do not preach the gospel!" (1 Cor. 9:16). Because of how the plaque is placed, every minister who stands in that pulpit touches it while he or she preaches. It is there as a reminder that the minister's job is not to tell stories or jokes or good moral points; it is to preach the gospel of Jesus Christ. My prayer and charge for you is that your ministry will be marked by, "Woe to me if I do not preach the gospel!" Preach the good news of Jesus Christ, sisters. By your life and doctrine, proclaim him as Savior.

> And when you are done serving him in this world, the words you will have waited to hear, will come because of who he is for us and what he has done through us: "Well done, good and faithful servant!" (Matt. 25:21)

Now go in peace to love and serve the Lord. In the name of Jesus Christ, amen.

> *Let nothing disturb thee; Let nothing dismay thee: All things pass; God never changes. Patience attains all that it strives for. He who has God finds he lacks nothing: God alone suffices.*
>
> ST. TERESA OF AVILA[2]

ACKNOWLEDGMENTS

This book is the fruit of ten years of prayer, study, and conversations with many individuals whom I would like to thank for their contribution to this project. The following people have helped shape this book in one way or another: Leslie Ann Jones, Meredith Teasley, Hayden Walker, E. Randolph Richards, Denise George, LeAnn Little, and Deborah Leighton. Frank Thielman, my former professor at Beeson Divinity, gave me early access to his commentary on Romans for this book. Bryan Gill read the first four chapters and provided helpful comments. Craig Keener graciously sent me a copy of his book *Paul, Women and Wives: Marriage and Women's Ministry in the Letters of Paul* to help me with the writing of this book. Gerald R. McDermott, a professor and colleague at Beeson, listened to me talk about the project and gave advice and encouragement throughout the process. Collin Hansen, whose office is located on the same hall as my office, listened and gave wisdom to this first-time author. I am indebted to all these people for their acts of kindness.

I am especially thankful for Jamie Flowers and Meredith Jackson for being part of my initial test group and allowing me to mentor them. Watching them mature in their faith and callings has been one of my greatest joys. I am grateful to Timothy George, dean of Beeson Divinity School, for his constant encouragement. Sabina Cook has been a faithful companion and friend. She read, edited, and provided feedback to my book proposal and entire book and has been a wonderful conversation partner. Joseph R. Dodson read the book and provided helpful comments. I am grateful for Barbara Pemberton, my mentor and professor at Ouachita Baptist University, who invited me to Ouachita in 2015 to lead a retreat for young college women called to ministry. This opportunity allowed me to try out some of my material and refine some areas of my exegesis.

Publishing with Zondervan Academic would not have been possible without the help of Paul House, another former professor at Beeson, who gave them my book proposal. I am truly appreciative of Dr. House for helping a former student. The folks at Zondervan have been wonderful to work with, especially my editor, Ryan Pazdur. Ryan believed in this project and was willing to take a risk on me, an unpublished author. I am grateful for his patience and collaboration. I am also grateful to Harmony Harkema for her contribution to this project. This book is what it is because of these people and others I may have failed to mention.

Those who deserve the most thanks are those closest to me: my family. I would not be where I am today without the loving kindness of my parents, Mark and Sherry Lindsey. They introduced me to my Savior, Jesus Christ, and reared me in church. They taught me Scripture, and their prayers and encouragement girded me. When I felt called to ministry, they were the ones who encouraged me to say yes to Jesus and his call, even if I couldn't see the end result.

Last, I'd like to thank the most important person in my life, my husband and best friend, Osvaldo. I married a man who is always encouraging and supportive of me in ministry. Osvaldo has patiently listened to me talk through this book and has been an excellent conversation partner. As a New Testament scholar, he has been an invaluable resource of biblical and theological knowledge. Osvaldo also read and edited the entire book, giving careful attention to detail. Of course, any remaining shortcomings are mine. Together, he and our son, Philip, have carved out time and space for me in our home to write and have made sacrifices to see this project brought to completion. Osvaldo, I dedicate this book to you, for without you this book simply would not be. *Con todo mi amor.*

NOTES

Introduction

1. Brevard S. Childs, *Old Testament Theology in a Canonical Context* (Philadelphia: Fortress Press, 1985), 124.

2. Thomas C. Oden, *Pastoral Theology: Essentials of Ministry* (San Francisco: HarperOne, 1983), 18.

3. Søren Kierkegaard, *Journals and Papers* I 1030 (Pap. IV.A.164) n.d., 1843.

4. Robert Smith Jr., *Doctrine That Dances* (Nashville: B&H Publishing, 2008), 10.

Chapter 1

1. Thomas F. Torrance, *The Christian Doctrine of God, One Being Three Persons* (New York: Bloomsbury T&T Clark, 2016), 4.

2. Ibid., 5.

3. John H. Walton, *Genesis* (Grand Rapids: Zondervan, 2001), 147–52, 181–87.

4. John I. Durham, *Exodus* (Waco: Word Books, 1987), 37–39.

5. Email from Leslie Ann Jones on Nov. 9, 2017.

6. Ex. 14:11–12; 16:2; 20; 17:2–3; Num. 11:1–6; 14:2; 16:41.

7. Deut. 31:23; Josh. 1:9.

8. As an exercise, count how many times Moses is described this way in the book of Joshua. What do you observe?

9. John Calvin, *Institutes of the Christian Religion*, ed. John T. McNeill, 2 vols. (Philadelphia: Westminster, 1960), 1:108.

10. See 1 Sam. 23:2–5; 30:8; 2 Sam. 2:1.
11. *Dietrich Bonhoeffer* Works, eds. Victoria J. Barnett and Barbara Wojhoski, trans. Isabel Best, vol. 13 (Minneapolis: Fortress, 1996–2013), 350.
12. See also Jer. 14:13–16; 23:1–40; 27:16; 28:5–17; 29:31–32.
13. See Jer. 15:15–21 and 20:7–11.
14. Episcopal Church. Protestant Episcopal Church in the Confederate States of America. *The Book of Common Prayer and Administration of the Sacraments and Other Rites and Ceremonies of the Church: Together with the Psalter or Psalms of David According to the Use of the Episcopal Church* (New York: Church Publishing Incorporated, 2007), 520.

Chapter 2

1. Smith Jr., *Doctrine That Dances*, 23.
2. John 4:34; 5:23–24, 30, 36–38; 6:29, 38–39, 44, 57; 7:16, 18, 28–29, 33; 8:16, 18, 26, 29, 42; 9:4; 11:42; 12:44–45, 49; 13:20; 14:24; 15:21; 16:5; 17:3, 8, 18, 21, 23, 25; 20:21.
3. For something similar, see John 12:44–45.
4. Often the Gospel writers said of Jesus that he was "full of the Holy Spirit" or the Holy Spirit was on him.
5. The concept of Jesus as Prophet, Priest, and King stems from the Reformed tradition.
6. Walter Bauer, *A Greek-English Lexicon of the New Testament and Other Early Christian Literature*, 3rd ed. Rev and ed. Frederick William Danker (Chicago: University of Chicago Press, 2000), 698.
7. For a fuller discussion, see Philip H. Towner, *The Letters to Timothy and Titus*, The New International Commentary on the New Testament (Grand Rapids: Eerdmans, 2006).
8. Philip H. Towner, *The Letters to Timothy and Titus* (Grand Rapids: Eerdmans, 2006), 479.
9. Ibid., 584.

Chapter 3

1. To learn more about women in church history, see Diana Lynn Severance's two books: *Feminine Threads: Women in the Tapestry of Christian History* (Fearn, Scotland: Christian Focus, 2011) and *Her-Story: 366 Devotions from 21 Centuries of the Christian Church* (Fearn, Scotland: Christian Focus, 2016). Also see Ruth A. Tucker and Walter L. Liefeld, *Daughters of the Church: Women and Ministry from New Testament Times to the Present* (Grand Rapids: Zondervan, 1987).

2. William J. Webb, *Slaves, Women & Homosexuals: Exploring the Hermeneutics of Cultural Analysis* (Downers Grove: IVP, 2001), 76–81.

3. Craig Keener, "Women in Ministry," *Two Views on Women in Ministry*, eds. James R. Beck and Craig L. Blomberg (Grand Rapids: Zondervan, 2001), 25-79.

4. The NIV translation doesn't capture the emphasis of the Hebrew as well here.

5. Trent C. Butler, *Judges* (Nashville: Thomas Nelson, 2006), 84.

6. The NIV translates this as "leading."

7. The NIV says, "She sent for Barak."

8. K. Lawson Younger, Jr., *Judges and Ruth*, The NIV Application Commentary (Grand Rapids: Zondervan, 2002), 141.

9. Butler, *Judges*, 84, 95; and Daniel I. Block, *Judges, Ruth* (Nashville: B&H, 1999), 199–200. (Also see Younger, *Judges and Ruth*, 141.)

10. Keener, "Women in Ministry," 33.

11. Paul R. House, *1, 2 Kings* (Nashville: B&H, 1995), 384, and Andrew E. Hill, *1 & 2 Chronicles* (Grand Rapids: Zondervan, 2003), 621.

12. August H. Konkel, *1 & 2 Kings* (Grand Rapids: Zondervan, 2006), 649.

13. Hill, 633.

14. Konkel, 635.

15. Hill, 622.

16. Ibid., 621.

17. House, 385.

18. Douglas Stuart, *Hosea-Jonah*, eds. David A. Hubbard and Glenn W. Barker (Nashville: Thomas Nelson, 1987), 260.

19. Stuart, 262.

Chapter 4

1. Acts 2:17–21.
2. Joel Green, *The Gospel of Luke* (Grand Rapids: Eerdmans, 1997), 87.
3. Ibid., 84.
4. Ibid., 78.
5. Ibid., 86.
6. Ibid., 92.
7. Ibid.
8. Ibid.
9. Ibid., 96.
10. Ibid., 101.
11. Ibid., 105.
12. Ibid., 317.
13. Craig Keener, *Acts: An Exegetical Commentary* (Grand Rapids: Baker, 2013), 3:2810.
14. Acts 18:18, 19, 26; Rom. 16:3; and 2 Tim. 4:19.
15. Keener, *Acts*, 3:2809.
16. Craig Keener, *Paul, Women and Wives: Marriage and Women's Ministry in the Letters of Paul* (Grand Rapids: Baker, 2004), 241.
17. See 1 Timothy 3:11. "In the same way" Paul is talking about female deacons. See also Andreas J. Köstenberger, *Commentary on 1–2 Timothy & Titus* (Nashville: Holman, 2017), 126.
18. Douglas Moo, *The Epistle to the Romans* (Grand Rapids: Eerdmans, 1996), 914.
19. Keener, *Paul, Women, and Wives* (Grand Rapids: Baker, 2004), 240.
20. For example, see Richard N. Longenecker, *The Epistle to the Romans* (Grand Rapids: Eerdmans, 2016), 1064; and Moo, 913.
21. Longenecker, 1064–65.
22. Ibid.
23. Gerhard Kittel, ed. *Theological Dictionary of the New Testament* (Grand Rapids: Eerdmans, 2006), Vol. 1, 422.
24. Other apostles include James (Gal. 1:19), Barnabas, Silvanus, and Apollos (1 Cor. 4:6, 9; 9:5–6; 1 Thess. 2:6–7).

Chapter 5

1. Rom. 16:21; 1 Cor. 4:17; 16:10; 2 Cor. 1:1, 19; Phil. 1:1; 2:19, 22; 1 Thess. 3:2; 6.
2. Linda Belleville, "Teaching and Usurping Authority: 1 Timothy 2:11–15," *Discovering Biblical Equality: Complementarity Without Hierarchy*, eds. Ronald W. Pierce and Rebecca Merrill Groothuis (Downers Grove: IVP, 2005), 206–7.
3. See Bruce Winter, *Romans Wives, Roman Widows: The Appearance of New Women and the Pauline Communities* (Grand Rapids: Eerdmans, 2003).
4. Ibid., 1–14, 97–140.
5. Ibid., 98.
6. I. Howard Marshall, *A Critical and Exegetical Commentary on The Pastoral Epistles* (New York: T&T Clark, 1999), 454.
7. Marshall, 777.
8. Andreas J. Köstenberger, *Commentary on 1–2 Timothy and Titus* (Nashville: B&H Publishing, 2017), 112–113.
9. Ibid., 114, 117.
10. Ibid., 115.
11. Ibid., 113.
12. Towner, 239.
13. Ibid., 220.
14. Belleville, 211–217.
15. Marshall, 459.
16. Payne, 391.
17. Marshall, 453.
18. Ibid., 454.
19. Köstenberger, 114.
20. Ibid., 117.
21. Ibid.
22. Ibid., 118–119.
23. Ibid., 117.
24. William J. Webb, *Slaves, Women & Homosexuals: Exploring the Hermeneutics of Cultural Analysis* (Downers Grove: IVP, 2001), 113.

25. Marshall, 460–63.

26. Webb, 114.

27. Keener, "Women in Ministry," 61–63.

28. See a listing of scholars who hold this view in William Mounce's commentary on the Pastoral Epistles in the *Word Biblical Commentary* (Nashville: Thomas Nelson, 2000), 145.

29. Towner, 235.

30. Commonly attributed to St. Augustine.

Chapter 6

1. Frank Thielman, *Ephesians* (Grand Rapids: Baker, 2010), 203, 273.

2. Paul R. House, *Old Testament Theology* (Downers Grove: InterVarsity Press, 1998), 222, 230, 263.

3. Childs, 125, 132.

4. Thielman, 273.

5. Gordon Fee, *The First Epistle to the Corinthians* (Grand Rapids: Eerdmans, 1987), 505-6.

6. Thielman, 274.

7. Ibid., 275.

8. Ibid., 277.

9. Spoken during a Reformation Heritage Lecture given at Beeson Divinity School on Oct. 31, 2017.

10. Moo, 663.

11. Ann L. Bowman, "Women in Ministry," *Two Views on Women in Ministry*, 271.

12. Paraphrase of "What's in a name? That which we call a rose by any other word would smell as sweet." William Shakespeare, *Romeo and Juliet* (New York: Houghton Mifflin Company, 1911), 28.

13. Thielman, 281, and Marcus Barth, *Ephesians: Introduction, Translation and Commentary on Chapters 4–6*, (London: Yale University, 1974), 483.

14. Barth, 479.

15. See Thielman, 277–80.

16. See Kenneth C. Kinghorn, *Discovering Your Spiritual Gifts* (Grand Rapids: Zondervan, 1984); Bruce L. Bugbee, *Discover Your Spiritual*

Gifts the Network Way (Grand Rapids: Zondervan, 2005); and William J. McRae, *The Dynamics of Spiritual Gifts* (Grand Rapids: Zondervan, 1983).

17. Email from Leslie Ann Jones on Nov. 9, 2017.
18. Barth, 481.

Chapter 7

1. Email from Meredith Teasley on June 6, 2017.
2. Email from Hayden Walker on May 31, 2017.
3. https://www.beesondivinity.com/articles/a-biblical-pattern-for-theological-education. Also, see Paul House's book *Bonhoeffer's Seminary Vision: A Case for Costly Discipleship and Life Together* (Wheaton: Crossway, 2015).

Conclusion

1. C. S. Lewis, *The Horse and His Boy* (New York: HarperCollins, 1954), 164.
2. *The Complete Works of St. Teresa of Avila*, ed. and trans. E. Allison Peers (London: Burns & Oats, 2002), 288.

9 780310 532187